Treaties
Nez Perce Perspectives

Treaties
Nez Perce Perspectives

The Nez Perce Tribe

Λ

Environmental Restoration & Waste Management Program

in association with

The United States Department of Energy and Confluence Press

Publication of *Treaties: Nez Perce Perspectives* is made possible, in part, by funding from the U.S. Department of Energy under cooperative agreement #DE-FC06-92RL 12539 and the Nez Perce Tribe Environmental Restoration and Waste Management Program.

A special thanks to the following list of contributors:
(in alphabetical order)

Horace Axtell, Kristie Baptiste, Dave Cummings, Rick Eichstaedt, Carla HighEagle, Dave Johnson, Julie Kane, Diane Mallickan, Allen Pinkham, Julie Simpson, Antonio Smith, Patrick Sobotta, Angela Sondenaa, William Swagerty, Rev. Henry Sugden, and Rebecca Miles Williams

The book was designed by Brian Kolstad and Grant Bathke.

First Edition 10 9 8 7 6 5 4 3 2 1

ISBN: 1-881090-45-0 (paper)
          1-881090-46-9 (cloth)

Library of Congress Control Number: 2002116613

DEDICATION

We issue this book to commemorate and honor our ancestors: both those who signed the treaties under coercion and duress to prevent war and those who refused to sign the treaties, and, in so doing, gave up their lives defending the lands now presumed lost because of those "agreements." We consecrate this book to all *Nimiipuu*, living and dead, past and present, counting those individuals still exiled into other lands and among other tribes, including the Chief Joseph Band living on the Colville and Umatilla reservations, and not least those exiles about whom we may not yet know. It is these exiled Nez Perces whom the treaties have most affected by alienating them from their homeland and separating them from their own people.

The decisions our ancestors made regarding the treaties were perversely difficult to make and, consequently, frustrated and divided our people. It is fitting, therefore, that we should take this occasion to honor all our leaders and ancestors, who did the very best they could to act on our behalf in dangerous and confusing times. It is the very generations who live today, and who will be born, that they continually bore in mind. They knew their actions would decide, in a future they would not and could not entirely see, our very survival as a people.

FOREWORD

First, thank you for taking the time to read these words.

These words are important because they reflect the true perspectives of many Nez Perce people. Although there are many books, articles, and other materials written by individuals who have studied one or more aspects of the Nez Perce Tribe, until now the Tribe has not taken on the project of formally writing and sharing with the general public the views of the Nez Perce people concerning our own history and our own culture.

It is time.

In these days of uncertainty and reflection, it is wise to call upon the wisdom of our forebears. Our ancestors lived through many tragedies, struggled with unwelcome, heart-wrenching dilemmas, and witnessed the rapid destruction of their world. But the Nez Perce people are survivors. We have learned from our experiences and we are stronger for it. This book reveals not only the Nez Perce past but also the Nez Perce present. It documents some of our current activities and the collective hope we share for future generations.

One thing we ask. Each reader should understand that this book is in no way a legally binding document. As a tribe we have collectively authored this book exclusively for educational purposes. The book presents some (but by no means all) Nez Perce perspectives regarding treaties and their impact upon us as a people. In no sense is it a treatise on American Indian Law even as it pertains to us. American Indian law changes constantly. On the other hand, this book does present a snapshot of the history of the law and how it impacts our tribe today. Because Indian Law will continue to evolve as tribes continue to assert their sovereignty, many of the issues present today may appear in a different light next year, next week—or even tomorrow.

Enjoy the book. We hope that it will open your heart and your mind to the personalized historical events and time-honored beliefs of the *Nimiipuu* and the strong resolve that we, as a tribe, have for meeting, head on, events yet to unfold. It is with great pride that I write these words.

Sam Penney, Chairman
Nez Perce Tribal Executive Committee

TABLE OF CONTENTS

Preface.. x

Chapter 1   Nez Perce Origins.. 2

Chapter 2   First Contact and First Treaties 18

Chapter 3   Early Federal Indian Policy.. 24

Chapter 4   Expanded Western Settlement and Federal Treaties 34

Chapter 5   Allotment Era 50

Chapter 6   Shifting Winds of Modern Federal Indian Policy................................... 58

Chapter 7   Hunting, Fishing, Pasturing, and Gathering 70

Chapter 8   The Nez Perce Tribe Today 86

Appendix 1   A Nez Perce Creation Story 112

Appendix 2   Treaty of 1855.. 116

Appendix 3   Treaty of 1863.. 120

Appendix 4   Treaty of 1868.. 125

Appendix 5   The Dawes Act.. 127

Appendix 6   1893 Allotment.. 131

Appendix 7   Nez Perce Tribe Organization Chart 2002 138

Glossary of Terms 139

Selected Bibliography... 143

PREFACE

As we begin the 21st century, almost 150 years after the 1855 signing of the first treaty between the Nez Perce Tribe (*Nimiipuu*) and the United States, the experience of social holocaust still lingers in our memories and is evident in nearly every aspect of our daily lives. The treaties were not only the cause of the loss of our land: they laid the foundation for our present-day legal status and our economic survival. The ebb and flow of their effects haunts each Nez Perce individual and the Tribe as a whole in different but profound ways.

Treaties were not something that we sought.

Nevertheless, our ancestors understood that some level of legal protection of rights could only be obtained by signing treaties. Treaties were typically signed under relentless pressure from federal officials who wanted to somehow legitimize the invasion and theft of our land. Often these "agreements" were signed only because they were the sole means of preventing bloodshed. The treaties almost always resulted in the loss of immense portions of our homelands. In some cases, we were removed to desolate areas of the country where many of our people died.

The treaties did not bestow to us, either as a tribe or as individuals, any rights that we, as Nez Perce, had not previously enjoyed. Rather, our leaders wanted to insure that we would always retain as many of our former rights as possible. These rights included hunting, fishing, pasturing, and gathering in all of our usual and accustomed places, regardless of new reservation boundaries. These rights also included basic human rights including freedom of speech, freedom to travel, and freedom to practice, without interference, our aboriginal customs and our own religion.

The driving forces behind the treaties and the social and political results that divided us were both physical and spiritual. As *Nimiipuu*, as *Cupnitpelu*, we would never be the same people again after the making of the treaties. The separation from our homelands in the beautiful mountains of the Seven Devils, the Wallowas, the Bitterroots, and the Blues is a loss we still feel keenly today. Although many of our traditional homelands remain in the public domain under the stewardship of the United States Forest Service, Bureau of Land Management, and other agencies, too often Indian people have been (and continue to be) treated as intruders or outsiders in our own ancestral places.

To those who do not know the complete story of the treaties, it may appear that great benefits were bestowed upon enrolled tribal members who reside on the reservation. In harsh reality, the *Nimiipuu* retained only a small portion of our immense former wealth. After the implementation of the Dawes Act of 1887, which placed individual tribal members on allotted acreages to farm, there were very few large horse herds left to accomplish the tasks of our former life. Our hunting and fishing rights were ignored, dishonored, and disrespected, and, in fact, it was not until John McConville's 1943 arrest for fishing without a license, and David Arthur's 1951 arrest for allegedly shooting a deer "out of season" that the courts helped turn the tide in favor of Nez Perce Treaty rights. The distance between the Treaty of 1855 and David Arthur's 1951 arrest is almost a century.

This same social stigma of "outsider" was also placed on those who practiced our native religion. On the Nez Perce Reservation, it was not until 1975 that our native beliefs resurfaced from the underground back out into the open. Our Nez Perce lifeways exist only because of the sacrifices and persistence of our tribal spiritual leaders, elders, political leaders, teachers, grandparents, fishermen, hunters, and gatherers. These people (and many other unnamed tribal members) have passed down the knowledge of their livelihoods to our successive generations. Without them, we might have lost all tribal cultural patterns.

Some people wrongly believe that the treaties between the federal government and Indian tribes are no longer binding and therefore should have little or no influence on the ways that federal and tribal government agencies deal with each other. Federal court rulings, however, along with acts of Congress and Presidential executive orders, have consistently validated and confirmed, time and again, that these treaties and the rights we reserved in them are just as valid and just as important today as they were at the time when their negotiations took place. The treaties of the United States of America are the supreme law of the land: older than the states themselves and as valid as the Constitution of the United States.

Of course, bereft of social and cultural history, legal history is incomplete and impossible to understand. Social and cultural history is best told by those it directly involved. This book attempts to share some of our history by providing readers with a glimpse of what the treaties did to the Nez Perce and what those "agreements" really meant and what our ancestors intended them to accomplish. We believe the tribal community, surrounding non-Indian communities, U.S. government agencies, and the general public can benefit greatly from a more thorough education about the rights of the Nez Perce people. Through the publication and distribution of this book, we hope that our tribal members, our neighbors, and those who may never have set foot on our land will gain an increased understanding of our home, our culture, our jurisdiction, and our rights.

By sharing the Nez Perce Tribe's experiences, we hope to convey to readers everywhere the immense responsibilities placed upon tribal governments and tribal communities. We hope you enjoy this book and gain a greater sense of the important roles tribal governments play within the context of the United States of America.

ACKNOWLEDGEMENTS

Publication of this book would have been impossible without the dedicated efforts of the editing team of the Environmental Restoration and Waste Management Program (ERWM) of the Nez Perce Tribe under the direction of Patrick Sobotta and the Nez Perce Tribe Office of Legal Counsel under the direction of Julie Kane and team leaders Carla HighEagle and Rebecca Miles-Williams. The editing team included Kristie Baptiste-Eke, Judit German-Heins, Dan Landeen, John Stanfill, Julie Simpson, Diane Mallickan, Julie Kane, Rick Eichstaedt, Justine Miles, Sandra Lilligren, and Antonio Smith. This group was responsible for the overall writing, editing, layout, design, and publishing of the final document.

This document would not have reached completion without the support of the Nez Perce Tribal Executive Committee Chairman, Samuel N. Penney, and members Wilfred A. Scott, Julia A. Davis, Jaime Pinkham, Simone Wilson, Arthur M. Taylor Jr., James L. Holt, Anthony Johnson, Del T. White, Jake Whiteplume, Justin Gould, and Jennifer Oatman-Brisbois. Certainly, too, this book would never have become a reality without the assistance of tribal elders who provided us with a clearer understanding of the past and a vision of the future of the Nez Perce Tribe and its people. We thank those elders and other tribal members who were interviewed for this publication.

We also thank those who assisted with research and gave us access to information, including the Nez Perce Tribe Office of Legal Counsel, Marlene Trumbo, Ira Jones, Allen V. Pinkham, Sr., Allen Slickpoo, Sr., Jason Lyon, JoAnn Kauffman, Otis Halfmoon, Robert Applegate, Dave Johnson, and Michael J. Penney.

Last but not least, we are grateful for the technical support provided by Lilisa Moses, Candace Greene, Justine Miles, Antonio Smith, and April Shell. We would like to thank those organizations and their staffs who assisted us in finding materials to be included in this publication, particularly the Nez Perce National Park Service, Lewis-Clark State College, Nez Perce Tribe Cultural Resources Program, Water Resources, Land Services, and the Environmental Restoration and Waste Management Program.

Brooke Baptiste is the Nez Perce artist responsible for some of the black and white artwork throughout the book. These drawings previously appeared in another Nez Perce publication *Salmon and His People: Fish and Fishing in Nez Perce Culture.* Carolynne Merrell provided the pictographs that appear on this page and throughout the book.

Diminishment Map

The Nez Perce historically hunted and fished on land that totaled between 13 and 15 million acres. The federal government set aside 7.5 million of those acres for the Nez Perce in the Treaty of 1855. This reservation was diminished to 750,000 acres as a result of the Treaty of 1863. The Dawes Allotment Act in 1887 further reduced Nez Perce ownership to 250,000 acres while opening the remaining 500,000 acres to white settlement.

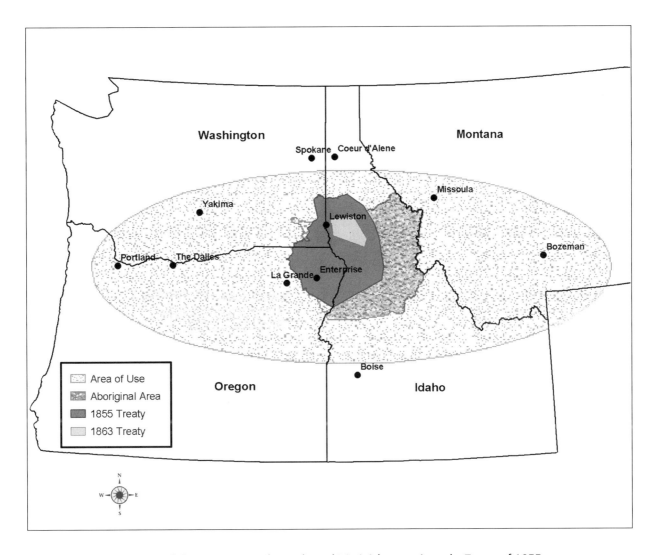

Territory of the Nez Perce Tribe and Land Diminishment since the Treaty of 1855.

Chapter 1

Nez Perce Origins

As Indian people we figured out when the times are that the fish come up the river. We would hear stories about tribal members that would go upriver below Selway Falls. They would just camp there waiting. They would send a guy to sit post and wait for them. The fish used to come so strong that you could hear them coming. It was just like when today you see the jet boats splash the water. That is what the salmon used to do. It was almost like rain, they would say. You could see them coming. They said that you could almost walk across on their backs, there were so many. They would run down there and pull out as much as they needed. That was all. Let the others go up the river to produce. . . .

I notice when I go fishing in the springtime, up in the creeks there are hardly any trout or even suckers. It seems like all the fish are getting bad. We used to catch chiselemouth down here and our people used to eat them—suckers, eels and everything. Now it's just a good thing to get an eel. The eels used to come up here, but they don't anymore. I remember we would go down to the Lewiston dam with my uncle, and we would sneak down there and get a sack of eels. They said it was against the law, but we went down there anyway.

Horace Axtell

We fish the same rivers our grandfathers fished long before the arrival of Columbus. We dig roots in meadows our grandmothers harvested before the rise of the Roman Empire. We live in the places our ancestors called home before the great pyramids of Egypt were built. Our land defines the Nez Perce Way.

In one of the first books written from the Nez Perce perspective, *Hear Me My Chiefs*, L.V. McWhorter records an oral interview with Howlis Wonpoon (or War Singer, also known as Camille Williams), a native linguist and interpreter who provided the following account about the antiquity of the tribe:

> On the North Fork of the Clearwater River a few miles below Bungalow Ranger Station, the footprints of a human are plainly seen, sunken into the basaltic rock formation. The tracks are those of a man running upstream. These footprints were made in a soft surface. How long since the change into hard basalt took place nobody knows. That man was older than the stone itself. On the Snake River there are stony tracks of a woman and a child. Also tracks at a bathing place near Fir Bluff, today a solid rock formation. All these we regard as of Nez Perce origin.

McWhorter also records some of the earliest stories of the Nez Perce—stories about a people who lived in the high mountains along the rivers of the Bitterroot country. *Cupnitpelu* (The Emerging or The Walking Out People) was one of the early names not only for the *Nimiipuu* but also for all Plateau peoples including the Umatilla, Yakama, Cayuse, Palouse, Walla Wallas, and some of the Warm Springs tribes. One of the Nez Perce creation stories tells us that our ancestors lived near the Salmon River, and as we grew more numerous we began to travel farther and farther—and to settle along other rivers. These stories serve as our aboriginal Bible. They explain our beginnings. Coyote, our teacher, also appears in a creation story about our beginnings in which he plays a significant role (Appendix 1). These stories and others, passed down for millennia to each generation through our oral tradition, help to preserve our values and the vital lessons we have learned

Petroglyphs near Buffalo Eddy on the Snake River. (Photo courtesy of Carolynne Merrell.)

I want you to understand that there was another aspect of life already here when the non-Indian people came to this country. It was a good life. Sure, we had our difficulties before the white man came, but they were difficulties that had more to do with the battling of the elements. In our stories we would learn how to survive the harsh conditions that could be imposed by the elements.

Allen Pinkham

from our land, and were not just for children or entertainment. We were originally the *Sahaptin* speaking peoples, placed here by Coyote. Creation stories, myths, and legends tell us of our humble beginnings, although they also remind us of much that we have learned from the creation and the creatures around us.

In a land of rolling hills, prairies, clear mountain streams, and deep canyons, we made our home. It was here, too, in this beautiful land, that we became a powerful nation. Our story, when written by others, however, too often focuses almost exclusively on the Nez Perce War of 1877, also known as the Chief Joseph War. By contrast, we understand that our story began long before these more recent events occurred and, perhaps most importantly, that our story continues to this day. Because of our strong oral tradition, we remember the lessons we learned along the mountain trails and on the prairies, and these teachings remain vital to us, to our very survival as the Nez Perce people.

The aboriginal Nez Perce Tribe occupied a territory that encompassed virtually all of what is now north central Idaho, northeastern Oregon, and southeastern Washington State. In the adjudication of Nez Perce claims for the taking of property without just compensation, the Indian Claims Commission determined that the Nez Perce Tribe once had exclusive use and occupancy of 13,204,000 acres of land.

Historically speaking, Nez Perce who lived in a given place were known to each other by the river drainage and the Nez Perce name for the area in which they lived. In addition to the geographical name of the

Historic Nez Perce village at Spalding next to the Clearwater River. (Photo courtesy of Nez Perce National Historical Park.)

place (such as *Lamaatta, Walwaama, Saqaanma,* or *Palutcpu*), these areas were also named for the leaders or headmen of that place. Today, bands are remembered by the oldest known leader of their given area or their last occupation prior to displacement. We refer, for example, to the Looking Glass Band, to the Whitebird Band, to the Joseph Band, to the Snake River Band, and to the Palouse Band. Most of the Nez Perce on the reservation today are Upriver (Kamiah and above), Downriver (Lapwai area), and *Aspacha* (Orofino area). Outside the reservation, many Nez Perce live on the Palouse.

Social interchange and trade were historically and prehistorically conducted among many of the bands throughout the Columbia River Basin. Many of the people divided into tribes today still have blood ties to members of other tribes as a result of ancestral intermarriages between bands

> "A delicate balance was maintained between land and the people..."

and tribes. Because intermarriage on the Plateau continues, the tribes in our area are still related by blood. The Nez Perces traditionally lived in small, semi-permanent villages scattered along major rivers and streams. There are more than 300 known Nez Perce village sites in the aboriginal areas of Oregon, Idaho, and Washington that encompass over 13.5 million acres. Economic viability dictated that the Nez Perce bands move in an annual gathering cycle, which meant that there were few permanent villages where people resided all year long. A delicate balance was maintained between the land and the people, and our social customs and religion prevented us from over-populating ourselves or over-exploiting our land resources. Our political organization was informal with the headmen of each area maintaining order. Territorial rights were honored and special permission had to be obtained to hunt, fish, or gather in another's territory.

The traditional social structure of the Nez Perce "tribe" consisted of villages, bands, composite bands, and the Tribe itself. Villages were often comprised of family and extended family groupings. We had (and needed) very little extended political organization beyond the band headmen and peace leaders who insured the safety and provisioning of the women, elderly, and children.

Leadership, on the other hand, was specialized with regard to function. We elected leaders for activities such as warfare, hunting, fishing, religion, conflict resolution, and healing. Councils existed at all levels of our political organization and exercised a dominant influence over the actions of individual leaders.

Individuals derived their tribal identities from the commonality of language, land, and family. As Nez Perce, we believed that an individual possessed the right to disagree with and remain unbound by the rule of the majority. (In one of our creation stories, for example, Chipmunk and Grizzly Bear ferociously debate the duration of Day and Night. Although Grizzly Bear loses the argument for "six months of day and six months of night," he nevertheless wins the right to live his life as he sees fit by sleeping, or hibernating during the winter months.) This simple individual right to conscientiously object to the majority opinion existed prior to the treaties and is still evident within the decision making process of the Tribe today. The Treaty of 1855 between the federal government and the Nez Perces was signed by sixty headmen, which indicates that there were at least sixty villages and bands of our people living as Nez Perce in the mid-nineteenth century just prior to the Civil War in the United States.

> "The arbitrary classification of the native peoples of the Americas into "tribes" was primarily a European convention..."

The arbitrary classification of the native peoples of the Americas into "tribes" was primarily a European convention, a convention that eventually proved politically advantageous to the United States government. By labeling major groups of people who inhabited a given geographical area as a "tribe," the nascent United States government could then justify dealing with each group separately. Such labeling had the desired effect of scattering and dividing the people and also resulted in the eventual degradation of a very strong indigenous Nez Perce culture.

For decades, explorers, missionaries, military men, historians, and anthropologists have purported to record our story. Yet we have maintained our own identity through our oral histories, our songs, our tales, our legends, our dances, and our religious and cultural ceremonies. Our identity and our story are written within our hearts and minds. It is the strength of our elders who carry our oral traditions and the spirit of our children that continue to bring life to us in full circles, circles that transcend the adversity and challenges of our changing society.

It is important that we acknowledge our pre-European-American history. Our oral history reminds us of our ancestral lives, but we sometimes forget the spiritual side of those lifeways. To some extent, the lives of our ancestors are recorded in the treaties. Our spiritual values related to hunting, fishing, and gathering are even reflected in the treaty language. The very purpose of protecting these rights was to safeguard our strong spiritual beliefs. Furthermore, by protecting in the treaties our right to choose and practice our spiritual beliefs, our ancestors were insuring, or at least attempting to insure, the survival of our native beliefs. For the Nez Perce, fishing, hunting, and gathering were and are religious activities, and our movement across the landscape, our road of life, was and remains the way we express our conception of the sacred cycle of life.

The values that sustain and drive Nez Perce society and culture today are essentially and fundamentally the same values that were important to us when the treaties were being negotiated. Although we have experienced changes over time, the ancient and unchanging identity of the Nez Perce in terms of beliefs, community, family, and religion continue to hold the strong fabric of our society and culture together. These are the foundations of our individual and collective Nez Perce identity, and they reside at the center of the way we view ourselves and our relationship to our surroundings.

Those who cut up the lands or sign papers for lands will be defrauded of their rights and will be punished by the Creator's anger. . . . You ask me to plough the ground! Shall I take a knife and tear my mother's bosom? Then when I die she will not take me to her bosom to rest ... Shall I dig under her skin for bones? Then when I die I cannot enter her body to be born again.

Smohalla, Prophet of the Wanapums and many other Northwest people including the Nez Perce.

Being a Native American, being Nimiipu. . . . *One word! But a word which reflects the teachings of my elders. Being* Nimiipu *was instilled in me with great care and with love by my grandfather and my grandmother. . . the importance of those lessons I must now pass on to our future generations. . . teachings of pride in who we are and a rich heritage, left in our care, by our ancestors. We must protect and maintain this heritage and keep a good self image.* Nimiipunawit *is an important and integral part of our being.*

Allen P. Slickpoo, Sr.

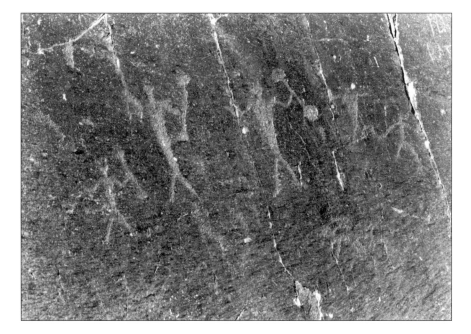

Petroglyphs near Buffalo Eddy on the Snake River. (Photo courtesy of Bruce Twitchell.)

SPIRITUALITY

As *Nimiipuu*, we have always practiced a belief system, or religion, uniquely our own. Many of our songs, prayers, dances, rituals, and ceremonies have been passed down through millennia. Others have been acquired more recently. Early explorers, fur traders, and missionaries frequently recorded their observations about our oral traditions and religious practices in so far as they could understand them. They also watched our people adopt new ways and adapt new ideas and new technologies. Many of those "new" ways and ideas, however, were not so different from our own. In Nez Perce culture, for instance, freedom of religion was neither spoken of nor justified: it was lived. Because of our interest in acquiring new ways of thinking and new technology, our people were intrigued by the beliefs of others. Even so, our ancestors did not intend that different beliefs should ever replace our own.

> "Because of our interest in acquiring new ways of thinking and new technology, our people were intrigued by the beliefs of others."

In 1869-70, the pressure of reformers and religious leaders in the East led President Grant to adopt a new 'peace' policy in dealing with the tribes. Under it, the government, violating the doctrine of separation of church and state, parceled out the reservations to different religious denominations, delegating to them the right to nominate the agents and administer tribal affairs. It was hoped that the churches would end the corruption and injustices that caused Indian hostility, as well as hasten the conversion of the Indians to Christianized farmers and their assimilation into white society.

Nez Perce Country: A Handbook for the Nez Perce National Park, Idaho, 1983.

Spirituality embedded itself in every aspect of traditional Nez Perce daily life. The early morning was greeted with prayer and song. The day ended with prayer and song. Each day's activities—whether digging roots, hunting, fishing, weaving (or creating any art), teaching children, or simply taking a sweatbath—were all conducted through spirituality. The success of the hunt or the harvest depended upon us demonstrating the proper respect for the Earth as our Mother. Our religion obliges us to avoid committing acts of greed or selfishness and to leave behind resources for others and thereby ensure next year's supply. Each year began by using all of the previous year's stores to avoid wasting the gifts of that ending year and thereby having to borrow from the future. Our relationship with native plants was engulfed in love and respect. Likewise, as we performed life-threatening activities—whether hunting buffalo on the Great Plains or fishing from the waterfalls on the Columbia River—love and respect for the gifts of the Creator and the creation guided our activities. Fishermen, for instance, had to commit themselves to waiting a required number of days after the runs began before attempting to fish. This waiting period ensured that humans and animals upstream would benefit from the patience of the fisherman. It also ensured that the annual spawning of the great salmon would take place. In this way, we secured the catch for successive years.

Every summer the various *Nimiipuu* bands gathered on the beautiful meadows and prairies of the Plateau. Each evening every family encamped nearby, including grandparents, aunts, uncles, children, and cousins, gathered to worship the Creator. They came together ceremonially to form a great circle, whereupon the Nez Perce men with their eagle fans would teach the young through songs. This circling made us strong and powerful. It helped us to maintain our unity.

As summer faded and the air began to turn cold and the people moved to lower ground, song and ceremony did not recede but continued. It was time now for the young people who had conducted their first successful hunts or harvests to both honor others and to be honored for their own accomplishments. Their families would hold large feasts to acknowledge their achievements, thereby insuring again that our resources would be protected and secured for the future. If we would take care of the Creator's gifts, then the Creator would take care of us. That was the sacred promise.

Spiritual gatherings continued throughout the cold season, including ceremonies to honor the winter solstice and other natural phenomena. Our Longhouses would be filled with Coyote teachings and tales of other cultural heroes, not to mention family stories that had been remembered and passed down the generations for hundreds of years. Our children were not taught categorically or by specialization of subject matter. Instead, spirituality was blended into every aspect of education as well as into all other aspects of life. Euro-Americans only learned of these ways because of the pressure placed upon our people during the treaty negotiations. It was then that our chiefs had to explain why they were unable to sign any treaty.

Over and over, our leaders patiently explained our traditional beliefs to

We do not wish to interfere with your religion, but you must talk about practical things. Twenty times over you have repeated the Earth is your mother, and that chieftenship is from the earth. Let us hear it no more, but come to business at once.

General Oliver O. Howard, Fort Lapwai, 1877

Our elders left us a beautiful example for us to follow. Many times the couples would be of two separate faiths. I remember my Auntie Vi and Uncle Jim. He went to the Longhouse and she went to the Church. If this was ever a conflict, we never knew about it. Freedom of religion was not intellectualized. It was lived. Political decisions were handled the same way. One spouse did not have the right to tell the other how to vote or what political views to take.

Diane Mallickan

Coyote plays a significant role in the creation story of the Nez Perce. (Photo courtesy of the Department of Energy.)

I am very thankful that the old ways are coming back to me as a young Nez Perce woman. We cannot choose the way we are brought up. The treaty era is a direct result of many of us being raised differently than traditional ways. Yet we knock each other down as if we had a conscious choice to suffer the consequences of treaties. I am very thankful that Wahlusat has survived and that those who protected it and kept it alive are now the teachers of this way. Without full acknowledgement of this way of life, then you have not quite understood what the War of 1877 was really about. I am very thankful for this deep understanding. This is something that no one can take away. It is in a place that is protected forever. So when the discussion of sovereignty is on the table or in the courts, I will never forget what sovereignty is really about, and there I will find it in that protected place, my heart.

Rebecca Miles Williams

government officials. Here, for example, is what Chief Joseph had to say:

> The earth and myself are of one mind. The one who has a right to dispose of the earth, is the one who created it. The earth is a part of my body. I belong to the land out of which I came. The earth is my mother. Never sell the bones of your father and mother. The earth is the mother of all people, and all people should have equal rights upon it. You might as well expect all rivers to run backward as that any man who was born free should be contented penned up and denied liberty to go where he pleases. Let me be a free man, free to travel, free to stop, free to work, free to trade where I choose, free to choose my own teachers, free to follow the religion of my fathers, free to talk, think, and act for myself—and I will obey every law or submit to the penalty.

The United States government used religion to divide and conquer the Nez Perce people by funding missionaries and their missions. Our ancestors made difficult choices to ensure the perpetuation of future generations. Whether they chose to sign the treaties or not, whether they chose to become "Christian" or not, it was the future and the survival of the *Nimiipuu* that each of them held in mind. Today, generations later, the Nez Perce share a diverse religious system that generally includes several denominations of Christianity (Presbyterians, Catholics, Methodists) and our native belief, *Walasat*, or Seven Drums.

The great diversity of religions we practice underscores the fact that we still firmly believe spiritual learning is central to the growth of individuals, our families, and our communities.

THE LONGHOUSE (KUHET INIIT)

The oldest known Nez Perce way of religious practice (*Walasat* or *Waashut*) nearly disappeared on the Nez Perce Reservation.

In the 1855 Treaty negotiations and many times thereafter, our chiefs and our leaders made it clear to the Euro-American military men and political leaders of the United States that our people would continue to practice our spiritual ways because those sacred ways are inseparable from the land we love and the water we use and the air we breathe. Unfortunately, to this day the connection that we believe exists between all things, what some call the sacred web of life, is still misunderstood. The idea of selling the land, or signing treaties, was as repulsive to us as the idea of selling a child. It was unthinkable.

This country holds your father's dying body. Never sell the bones of your father and mother.

Old Joseph

You white people get together, measure the earth, and then divide it. . . . part of the Indians gave up their land, I never did. The earth is part of my body; I belong to the land out of which I came. The earth is my mother.

Tuhuulhuulzute

Chief Joseph's Longhouse at Nespelem. (Photo courtesy of Nez Perce National Historical Park.)

One thing that the people of Joseph's Band and the White Bird Band always held is the religious observance of turning-around-oneself (ipnu-cilipt). They never failed to hold the ceremony day after day. Early in the morning they were off to dig. The women dug, until a little after noon, then in the afternoon they went home. They cleaned themselves, bathed, and dressed. Then they went to their religious services. They heard the sound of the drum and got started. They raised their hands and sang songs. When they were ready to do the religious rite, all who were going to take part in the worship held the tail feathers of eagles and kept time fanning the feathers as they rose up and down. There was another thing that these worshippers did. They had no rubbish outside. The earth was theirs and they always kept it clean. They respected the earth and never left anything untidy lying around.

Elizabeth Wilson, 1961

That is why prayers and hymns were translated in the Indian language, as this [translation] assisted the preservation of the language. It also brings to mind that this is how change occurred with regards to the instruments and practices of a religion: the people incorporated them into their belief system."

Margie Waheneka Palouse/Cayuse

All through the darkest decades in the aftermath of the 1877 War, the religion of our ancestors survived. Perhaps the most notable place of its continued practice was with Chief Joseph and his survivors on the Colville Reservation in northeastern Washington State. Perhaps because Catholicism had a larger influence there than it did on the Lapwai reservation, rigid criticism and hostility expressed toward our aboriginal religion and its practices was somewhat less common. Chief Joseph nevertheless observed and responded as follows when offered a mission for his Nez Perce band:

> We do not want churches because they will teach us to quarrel about God, as the Catholics and Protestants do. We do not want that. We may quarrel with men about things on earth, but we never quarrel about the Great Spirit.

These words gave guidance to those exiled people and credence to the continued legacy of the Longhouse despite their being in exile far from their beloved homeland. Historically, Longhouses were constructed of hides, or tule mats, but the photograph of a Longhouse on the previous page was taken at the turn of the century when such houses were commonly being made of canvas. After the introduction of sawmills, lumber was used to build a more permanent Longhouse, and in 1916 it also housed several Nez Perce families. Still standing, this Longhouse is a reminder of an earlier day when the predominant non-Indian sentiment was perhaps best expressed by Major Anderson of Fort Colville when describing Chief Joseph's people:

> Joseph and his band. . . . . they have been persistent in following their ancient traditions and indulging in their primitive customs. . . . They are strictly "blanket" Indians, and their dress on frequent occasions is hideous in appearance and possesses many of the characteristics of the Indian in the native state. On their small farms the government has erected comfortable and suitable housing, but none of them is ever occupied [for the past seven years].

In 1976, the Colville Tribe built a new Longhouse for the Joseph Band in the Nespelem District that is still active today. A short time later, the districts of Keller, Omak, and Inchelium also had Longhouses built in addition to their churches.

Nez Perce descendants on the Umatilla reservation in Oregon also maintained the *Walasat* practice in the midst of the Protestant and Catholic missionary movement. In the 1970s, *Walasat* practice was revived and made a strong comeback as young people began to ask their elders more about it. Margie Waheneka recalls, for instance, that the joining of the two beliefs, Waashut and Christianity, often became viable as one, or the other. Completely unknown to many outsiders (and even when acknowledged, often misunderstood) this joining was far more complementary than it was conflicting. The delicate balance of Indian spirituality and Christian practices has always been a pragmatic reality to most native peoples everywhere.

> "Meanwhile, the Presbyterian Church flourished on the Nez Perce Reservation where today there are still six churches."

Meanwhile, the Presbyterian Church flourished on the Nez Perce Reservation where today there are still six churches located throughout the area. This Christian influence overshadowed the Indian religion and in some ways the church *became* the Longhouse. However, for many years, it was only in private homes that the Nez Perce people would practice *Walasat* or other ceremonies known among the Plateau. This influence of the Presbyterian Church pervaded the reservation until the mid 1960s when the resurgence of traditional native practices made a national comeback.

The turning point on the Nez Perce Reservation came in 1975 when Horace Axtell was approached by a number of elders who were concerned about the funerals of those who were non-church members of the Tribe. These Nez Perce people had no one to bury them according

Annual religious celebration at Talmaks in 1915. Left to right: Josiah Redwolf, Sam Frank, Oliver Frank (Sam's son), Ben Penny Sr., Charles Amera, Francis McFarland, Nathanial Jabeth, David McFarland, Charles Williams, and William Moody. (Photo courtesy of Nez Perce National Historical Park.)

to their beliefs. About the same time, an elder who is now deceased, Elsie Frank, offered a small building adjacent to her home as a place to hold *Walaset* services.

For the Nez Perce, the centennial (or 100 year anniversary) of the 1877 War helped to change the attitude of a nation. To give further impetus to the recognition of our right to freedom of religion, state and federal laws began to reflect the wrongs stemming from the earlier decades of cultural genocide committed against Indians everywhere. The 1968 American Indian Civil Rights Act, for example, defended the right of tribal councils to restrict their reservations to native religions and practices at the "exclusion of all others." Few, if any, followed this legal route, partly because religious tolerance is part of our aboriginal tradition and forced exclusion is, generally speaking, not the "Indian Way." Consensus through a democratic process would have been far more acceptable to traditional people.

Slowly, all through the 1970s and 1980s, it became more acceptable to be buried in both the traditional *and* Christian religion on the Nez Perce Reservation. By the mid 1990s, the Nez Perce Tribal Executive Committee supported the rebuilding of a Longhouse by finding available tribal land and setting up a building fund. Thanks to tribal elders, employees, and community members, plans are underway to build a new Longhouse in hopes of accommodating this resurgence and revival of the Old Ways.

First Presbyterian Church at Kamiah, Idaho. (Photo courtesy of Nez Perce National Historical Park.)

NEZ PERCE AND CHRISTIANITY

The Reverend Henry Sugden provided the following information.

I n 1831 a group of four Nez Perce men traveled to St. Louis in search of "*timas akamkineekai*" (The Bible) and someone to instruct them in it. The Nez Perce had heard about this book from Lewis and Clark as well as some of the mountain men and trappers. While in St. Louis they visited William Clark who was now Superintendent of Indian Affairs. Of the four men known to have made the trip to Missouri, only Rabbit Skin Leggings survived the trip to return to present day Idaho. Two of the men died while in St. Louis, and another died from disease on the way home. Even Rabbit Skin Leggings was killed in a skirmish with the Blackfeet near Salmon Forks before he actually made it all the way home. It must have appeared to many Indians and non-Indians that their trip to St. Louis had been in vain. Gradually, however, the news of their trip was published in some eastern church magazines, which interpreted the story as a plea by the Nez Perce for Christian missionaries.

In 1834 a Methodist minister by the name of Jason Lee was the first to make the trip West. However, after settling in the Willamette Valley in western Oregon, Lee's interests turned to real estate and commerce. He became engaged in bringing in new immigrants. The next year, 1835, Reverend Samuel Parker and Dr. Marcus Whitman made an exploratory trip to the West. Whitman was so excited about the opportunities he perceived that he went back East and recruited other missionaries, including Reverend Henry Spalding and his wife, Eliza. Whitman married Narcissa Prentice and immediately headed west on the Oregon Trail with the Spaldings. Eliza and Narcissa became the first white women to cross the Rocky Mountains. The Whitmans established a mission in Walla Walla in what is now the state of Washington, and the Spaldings established a mission among the Nez Perce in Lapwai, Idaho, where they served for several years.

After the Civil War, the Union General Ulysses Grant was elected President. He instituted what was called his "peace policy" towards Native Americans in 1869. President Grant consulted with various church groups to produce recommendations for reservation and school officials. These recommendations resulted in Spalding's return to Lapwai as Superintendent of Education. He was to be assisted by Miss Sue McBeth who was a teacher and a fellow missionary.

Although by this time missionaries had been absent from our country for about twenty-four years, many of the Nez Perces had continued to hold Christian services and to follow the teachings of the missionaries in their absence. Sue McBeth was joined by her sister, Kate, and together they organized a Bible school to train Nez Perces ministers. In succeeding years churches were built in Kamiah, Spalding, Ahsahka, Stites, and Ferdinand.

In 1897, the churches decided to hold an annual camp meeting for two weeks during the Fourth of July. They chose a site near Craigmont, Idaho, known as *Talmaks*, which was located among the old growth Ponderosa and fir trees. This camp meeting continues to this day and gives the Nez Perce Christians a place to worship, to entertain visitors, and to live again somewhat in the style of their immediate ancestors.

Account of Nez Perce People by Horace Axtell

There's an old song that describes something our people figured out a long time ago. The description is based upon their observations. The song is about dawn. . .

the earth is turning,
so there will be a new day

That rotation made them understand that the earth moved and that the sun stood still.

How old is that song?

How long did they know this?

No one knows.

Our people had a connection to the earth and knowledge of the solar system for thousands of years.

They discovered the seasons, the foods: that they came at the same time each year. The four-legged ones were good to eat.

They established the ones that were good for food and the ones that weren't.

Then came the summer. After they picked the berries, they would dry them. The sun had to help them again. They learned that the sun was not just for light, but for drying foods also.

Fall was best for hunting, after the summer of plenty, but more importantly because the spring was busy with the young being born and that cycle of life. The fall also had its fish runs. The people have been camping along the rivers like this for as long as we've known. It was also the warmest place in the winter. Our people would gather tule and other reeds for the mats and baskets and other items that they needed. They repaired their clothes and tools in the winter. They learned the technology of fire to heat rocks for warmth and cooking, fire to burn out the meadows for better root digging and hunting. They learned to tan hides for clothing, to take sweatbaths, mudbaths, and medicines for healthy bodies, and they were the greatest of all botanists because they learned of all the root foods, which ones to eat, which ones were poisonous.

The old people were very intelligent and knew the natural world more intimately than we do today. In the days before all these changes, the people prepared ahead of time for things, not like today—rush or last minute.

There's been a drastic change in the way we live.

Our old people knew all about the shortest day of the year. After that day, the sun comes a little higher and it begins to get warmer with time. After that shortest day, it's time to start singing for the new foods. The people learned to respect these things because of the songs, prayers, and other teachings. The people were happy.

HINMAHTOOYAHLATKEKTH/YOUNG JOSEPH

(NEZ PERCE) 1879:

. . . I do not understand why nothing is done for my people. I have heard talk and talk, and nothing is done. Good words do not last long unless they amount to something. Words do not pay for my dead people. They do not pay for my country, now overrun by white people. They do not protect my father's grave. They do not pay for all my horses and cattle. Good words will not give me back my children. Good words will not give my people good health and stop them from dying. Good words will not get my people a home where they can live in peace and take care of themselves. I am tired of talk that comes to nothing. It makes my heart sick when I remember all the good words and broken promises. There has been too much talking by men who had no right to talk. Too many misrepresentations have come up between the white people about the Indians.

Treat all people alike. Give them the same law. Give them all an even chance to live and grow. All people were made by the same Great Spirit Chief. They are all brothers and sisters. The earth is the mother of all people, and all people should have equal rights upon it. You might as well expect the rivers to run backward as that any person who was born a free person should be contented when penned up and denied liberty to go where they please. If you tie a horse to a stake, do you expect it will grow fat? If you pen Indians up on a small spot of earth, and compel them to stay there, they will not be contented, nor will they grow and prosper. I have asked some of the great white chiefs where they get their authority to say to the Indians that they shall stay in one place while they see white people going where they please. They cannot tell me. When I think of our condition my heart is heavy. I see people of my race treated as outlaws and driven from country to country, or shot down like animals.

I know my race must change. We cannot hold our own with the white people as we are. We only ask an even chance to live as other people live. We ask to be recognized as people. We ask that the same law shall work alike on all people. If the Indians break the law, punish them by the law. If the white people break the law, punish them also. Let me be a free person—free to travel, free to stop, free to work, free to trade where I choose, free to choose my own teachers, free to follow the religion of my foreparents, free to think and talk and act for myself—and I will obey every law, or submit to the penalty.

Whenever the white people treat the Indian as they treat each other, then we will have no more wars. We shall all be alike—brothers and sisters of one father and one mother, with one sky above us and one country around us, and one government for all. For this time the Indian race is waiting and praying.

Josephy, Alvin M. Jr. *The Nez Perce Indians and the Opening of the Northwest*. Abridged Edition.
Lincoln: University of Nebraska Press, (1965). Reprinted above with the kind permission of the author.

CHAPTER 2

FIRST CONTACT AND FIRST TREATIES

Over the years, the courts have established a set of principles to interpret treaties. One of the most important of these principles is that the courts must interpret the treaties in the way the Indians must have understood them at the time... Treaties are just as valid today as they were 150 years ago.

Julie Kane

Treaties divided and scattered us, both physically and spiritually. They threatened to sever our spiritual connection with the land and fostered the division of our people into Christian and non-Christian, treaty and non-treaty, and finally, tribe and non-tribe.

Quote from Joseph Band, 1999

The Indian policy of the United States can be divided into six eras: (1) The Colonization Era (1492-1776), (2) The Relocation Era (1776-1880s), (3) The Allotment Era (1887-1930s), (4) the Indian Reorganization Era (1934-1960s), (5) the Termination Era (1960-1970s), and (6) the Self-Determination Era (1975 to the present).

The North American continent was first inhabited by hundreds of "tribes" and bands of native peoples later known as American Indians. These tribes had organized social, economic, and governmental structures to protect their villages and resources. Each tribe or nation controlled its own territory, developed its own cultural and social structures, spoke one of 250 languages, practiced its own religion, and developed medicines to heal its sick. Alliances, the first early form of treaties, were made between native nations with regard to trade, commerce, and territorial boundaries.

In the time immediately following European contact, the Indian nations in most cases far outnumbered the early colonists and developed good trade relations with them. Treaties and agreements were made between neighboring tribes and nearby European immigrants in which European goods were exchanged for land and friendship. Few (if any) European colonists would have survived without the support of the neighboring tribes. The European concept of private property—personal ownership of land and resources—conflicted with native beliefs and customs. Alliances with the various tribes soon became increasingly important to the European nations who sought to further colonize America.

The treaties between non-Indian settlers and Indian nations were important in establishing relationships with European countries, particularly Britain, Spain, and France. These early treaties were based on international laws that freely recognized the property rights and sovereignty of Indian tribes. The most basic principles of federal Indian law today can be traced directly to these early agreements, which were based on the international laws of nations that granted Indians the right to travel, the right to trade, the right to defend themselves, and the right of title to all lands in America belonging to the original inhabitants. The urgency and necessity of these alliances became even

The U.S. government considered Lawyer to be the head chief of the Nez Perce at the Walla Walla Treaty Council in 1855. (Photo courtesy of Washington State Historical Society, Tacoma)

more apparent in 1763 during what is called the French and Indian War in which the powerful Iroquois Confederacy assisted the British in defeating France for European control of the eastern seaboard.

Nez Perce Colonial Era (1805-1855)

A summary of some of the major events impacting Nez Perce tribal life will be briefly presented here to provide a backdrop to the negotiations of the treaties with the Nez Perce, whose Colonial Era occurred later than those of eastern and mid-western tribes. Much of the following information was provided by University of Idaho professor William R. Swagerty.

> "For all intents and purposes the first official agreement between the Nez Perce and the government of the United States occurred in 1805..."

For all intents and purposes the first official agreement between the Nez Perce and the government of the United States occurred in 1805 with the Lewis and Clark expedition. Lewis and Clark were official representatives of the United States and entered into a "peace and friendship" agreement with the Nez Perce and other tribes. The Nez Perce took this agreement very seriously and often referred to it in their subsequent negotiations with the federal government.

Prior to its treaty-making era with the United States government, the Nez Perce had extensive experience dealing with the non-Indian fur trappers, trading companies, missionaries, and immigrants to the Oregon and Washington territories. The Nez Perce, along with the Cayuse, Umatilla, Walla Walla, Yakama, and other bands along the Columbia River system and well into Montana, had long secured a large territory for their use and occupation. The relationship between Native Americans and the fur trading companies was fairly amicable because the fur traders depended upon the tribes to provide pelts.

The Nimiipuu have occupied this country since time immemorial. When the Corps of Discovery entered the territory of the Nimiipuu there was a great discussion about these alien beings.

Allen Pinkham

The fur trade, however, was generally unappealing to the Nez Perce who hunted bison, elk, moose, deer, and bear. Other Plateau tribes shared the Nez Perce view, and, consequently, the fur trade business, so successful elsewhere, was a failure in our region. Fort Nez Perce was only in business for three months before it closed. Nevertheless, the regional tribes found other types of trade to be socially beneficial. The Nez Perce and Cayuse, for example, had well defined trade routes and trade agreements with the lower Snake River Indians to the south.

During this early time, the Christian religion found its way to the Plateau tribes through the traders, although the traders noted that the tribes of our region already had a strong sense of spirituality and moral conduct. Traders also commented that we possessed astute business acumen and the ability to develop and negotiate strong trade agreements. These early trade agreements (or charters) held the companies responsible for treating the tribes humanely and with good judgment. The trading companies and forts established residency, and some non-Indian traders married tribal members to secure trade relations. Most tribal people frowned on those members who chose to reside near or within the forts.

Another significant factor that dramatically impacted tribal cultures was the introduction and spread of European diseases. Smallpox and cholera often advanced well ahead of the early traders. These lethal diseases spread quickly, often in epidemic proportions, along the coast and up the Columbia River and into Nez Perce country. By the year 1810 an epidemic had nearly wiped out the lower Columbia River bands, and the news of this catastrophe soon reached the upriver tribes. Some of the Columbia River tribes, including the Nez Perce, had already acquired Euro-American farming techniques from non-Indians, and, consequently, perceived these diseases as supernatural retribution for having violated Mother Earth by plowing fields.

Others saw the arrival of the diseases as the fulfillment of prophecies that foretold the turning of the earth and the coming of the white people. Tragically, the trading companies also introduced liquor—with devastating effects. Our people had no experience in dealing with this alien substance and absolutely no genetic tolerance for it. Alcohol and the many problems that accompanied it contributed heavily to the increasing and substantial mistrust between the tribes and the white people—and to the erosion of good will.

The introduction of Christianity and its blending into indigenous Plateau cultures also negatively impacted the Tribe. In the central area of Nez Perce Country, the establishment of chieftainships eventually came to be based upon conversion to Christianity. The missionaries played a dominant role in inducing immigrants to come West and homestead in the Idaho and Oregon territories. The fur trading companies and the early Methodist missionaries established the Red River School at Fort Vancouver to educate the sons of tribal chiefs in Christianity, the English and European languages, and European/British

After the Nez Perce had befriended the Lewis and Clark expedition, they never involved themselves as middlemen in the fur trade. The killing of small animals for goods didn't make much sense.

W.R. Swagerty

21

The earth was created by the assistance of the sun, and it should be left as it was... The country was made without lines of demarcation, and it is no man's business to divide it...The earth and myself are of one mind. The measure of the land and the measure of our bodies are the same...Understand me fully with reference to my affection for the land. I never said the land was mine to do with as I choose. The one who has the right to dispose of it is the one who has created it.

Chief Joseph

social customs in hopes of "civilizing" the tribes. The fur companies, however, were far from being totally supportive of this concept. After all, these corporations and their agents depended upon the Indians to supply furs, not to become farmers. Regardless, the federal government's desire to establish trade routes, settle international boundaries, and bring white immigrants West soon outweighed the needs of the fur companies. Some of the earliest Indian students to attend the missionary schools included Spokane Garry, Coutenais Pelly, Nez Perce Ellis, and Cayuse Pitt. Ellis was the grandson of Red Grizzly, the famed Nez Perce warrior and headman from the Salmon River country. Another prominent student was Elijah Hedding, son of Walla Walla chief, PeoPeoMoxMox. The missionaries also established a following of tribal people who were interested in learning the ways of the whites and acquiring new technology.

The early traders and the missionaries of the Presbyterian, Catholic, and Methodist churches also instituted a system of criminal punishment that included public floggings of Indian offenders. In this system white offenders and law breakers were turned over to whites and Indian offenders were turned over to the tribal leaders. In 1842, Reverend Elijah White, an Indian Agent for Oregon Country, formalized these laws and appointed a head chief and sub chiefs. Ellis was elected the first Nez Perce Head Chief. To put it mildly, this system of government was not one the tribe adopted easily or even willingly. Flogging Indians in public, when whites went unpunished for offenses against tribal members, made the role of Head Chief very unpopular. When a white man in California, for example, murdered Elijah Hedding in 1843, his father, PeoPeoMoxMox, sought justice for his son and his family only to find the white laws impossible to enforce. This event and other similar events resulted in the reluctance of the Cayuse and Walla Walla tribes to enter into any agreements whatsoever with the United States government.

By the 1830s and 1840s the Nez Perce, Cayuse, and Umatilla tribes, as well as others, had acquired great herds of horses and Spanish cattle and were considered among the wealthiest tribes in the Northwest. Those tribal members who resided near the missions also produced agricultural crops they traded to the incoming colonists who were then arriving in the territory. At first, the immigrants were too few to pose any real threat to the subsistence of the tribes and usually passed through to destinations farther west like the Willamette Valley in Oregon. The Nez Perce and other tribes soon established trade routes to exchange goods with immigrants and brought home livestock, cloth, farm implements, and firearms. The tribes felt caught between their desire to ply the growing trade with the immigrants and their alarm at the size of the trespass and their increasing annoyance with squatters. By 1843, what had begun as twenty to thirty new settlers a year had soon increased to 800, then to 1,000. This increase resulted in a growing friction—and lack of redress for offenses to both Indians and whites. In addition, the desire of white immigrants to own lands prompted them to call for the establishment of a territorial government in 1845 and then the passage of the Oregon Territorial Organic Act in 1848, which, nevertheless, clearly recognized rights of Indian title to the lands in question.

> "By 1843, what had begun as twenty to thirty new settlers a year had soon increased to 800, then to 1,000."

The Oregon Territorial Organic Act, along with the Washington Territorial Act and the Oregon Donation Act, led to further direct conflicts over land title between the Indian tribes and the white settlers. The coastal tribes who had negotiated treaties prior to the Walla Walla Treaty Council with various representatives of territorial governments found that despite all the talk, Congress failed to ratify the treaties. Consequently, many tribes became extremely suspicious of those who claimed to speak for the government and skeptically doubted whether a people with so many different representatives would honor the laws and treaties.

CHAPTER 3

EARLY FEDERAL INDIAN POLICY

Treaties created divisions between our people and [between other] aboriginal peoples of this continent. The divisions are apparent when we identify ourselves. The soyapos created tribes, groups, religion, bands, upriver and down river rivalry, boarding schools. Many families have been ostracized by decisions made by the federal government.

Lee Bourgeau

To me, it's our ancestors. What is encompassed in that treaty is what they did not want to give up as a people, what they held onto. That's the one thing to me that really stands out in the treaty, the desire to be ourselves.

Anthony Johnson

Most principles of federal Indian law today developed from early European contact with American Indians. As early as 1532, Spain determined that it could legally acquire Indian lands only and exclusively with the consent of the tribes themselves. As Felix S. Cohen notes, this Indian right of possession was also supported by Pope Paul III who stated

> Notwithstanding whatever may have been or may be said to the contrary, the said Indians, and all other people who may later be discovered by Christians, are by no means to be deprived of their liberty or the possession of their property, even though they be outside the faith of Jesus Christ; and that they may and should, freely and legitimately, enjoy their liberty and the possession of their property; nor should they be in any way enslaved; should the contrary happen, it shall be null and of no effect.

During the formative years of the United States, early federal leaders frequently expressed and declared their good intentions toward tribes. In Article III of the 1787 Northwest Ordinance, for example, the federal government promised that "utmost good faith shall always be observed towards the Indians; their lands and property shall never be taken from them without their consent." Prior to, during, and after the Revolutionary War, both colonial and federal leaders were also mindful of the increasing need and importance for peaceful relations with the tribes. "Securing the Friendship of the Indians," wrote Benjamin Franklin, "is of the greatest consequence for these Colonies."

Even individual tribes had enough military power and political authority reaching well into the late 1700s that the fledgling United States was relatively weak by comparison. After the Revolutionary War, rather than worry about troubles with the Indian tribes occupying the American continent, early federal leaders felt compelled to pursue peace and establish secure relationships with the tribes. Consequently, it was not until after the War of 1812 that the relationship between the United States government and the tribes began to sour.

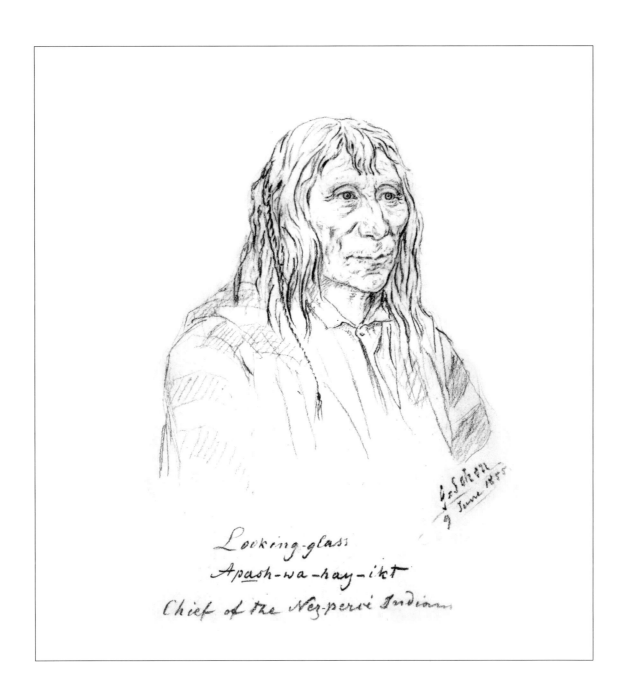

Looking-glass
Apash-wa-hay-ikt
Chief of the Nez-percé Indian

Looking Glass was a respected Nez Perce Chief who played a prominent role in the 1855 Walla Walla Treaty Council
(Photo courtesy of Washington State Historical Society, Tacoma)

The first and original principal of requiring the consent of the tribes before occupying and taking their lands was limited by Chief Justice John Marshall of the U.S. Supreme Court. In (*Johnson v. McIntosh*, 1823) Marshall determined that although tribes retained occupancy and use rights to their aboriginal lands, they were precluded from selling or ceding their lands to anyone other than the country that "discovered" them. Thus began the diminishment of true sovereignty for the Indian nations of North America.

"...Marshall conceived a definition of the tribes as something just slightly less than sovereigns."

Because of the tribes' growing dependence on the United States for their needs, rather than conceiving of Indian nations as foreign nations, Marshall conceived a definition of the tribes as something just slightly less than sovereigns.

In 1871, the practice of entering into treaties with Indian tribes was terminated by Act of Congress. The *need* for finalized agreements between the United States and Indian tribes, however, continued and persisted. The Nez Perce Tribe was party to one such agreement in 1893 (Appendix 6). The Allotment Act of 1887 described in Chapter 3 of this book also dealt a damaging blow to our tribal land base and resulted in the checkerboard pattern of land ownership shown elsewhere on the reservation map.

Nez Perce at Lewiston, Idaho in 1930. (Photo courtesy of Nez Perce National Historical Park.)

TRIBAL SOVEREIGNTY

To understand tribal governments and how they operate, we must first understand what tribal sovereignty means. Over many hundreds of years, tribal governments exercised their power by declarations of war, by defining and controlling territories, by managing and allocating resources, by punishing crimes, by regulating marriages, by adoption and by conducting various other aspects of their domestic relations. This form of government relied, not upon laws written in books or interpreted in courtrooms, but upon binding oral contracts and oral agreements. Such governments did not define their territories on maps and established no governmental offices. However, these complete governments nevertheless existed and flourished. Indian tribes possessed and exercised the same fundamental governmental powers as all other nations in the world did then and now.

Any foreign government that entered into treaties with the tribes, including the federal government of the United States, recognized the sovereign status of tribes. Indian tribes possessed inherent sovereign powers to the same extent and of the same kind possessed by other sovereign nations. These inherent powers existed because of the tribe's ability to act as a sovereign and the recognition of that ability by foreign sovereigns. In other words, Indian nations have always been

The treaty should never be abused. It should never be used for personal gain because that treaty was made for all of us, not one particular person. The treaty is something most of us really cherish. . . . I respect my treaty, I respect the people who made them, and I'm not going to go against it. Some of the signers were my relatives and I need to respect that. In the past, we had great roles of activism in our tribal communities. I think we are seeing a time when our tribal members have really grown numb to our ways and process of tribal government. We need to actively encourage tribal members to become involved in our political processes. If we begin empowering individuals themselves to pass on what they know to their children, then I think we can really start to perpetuate our culture. . . instill pride in them for who they are as human beings. Then I think we will begin to see some change in this tribe.

Roy White

Nez Perce General Council in Lapwai, Idaho. (Photo courtesy of Mae Taylor.)

To me, the trust with the United States is not what the Indians thought they bargained for. They bargained for trust that they thought would be carried out to the highest responsibility.

Del White

This Constitution, and the laws of the United States which shall be made in pursuance thereof; and all treaties made, or which shall be made, under the authority of the United States, shall be the supreme law of the land; and the judges in every state shall be bound thereby, anything in the Constitution or laws of any state to the contrary notwithstanding.

United States Constitution Article 6, Clause 2

Today, we look at how far the tribes have come, and I think that while that federal trust responsibility is there, I also think that the strength in tribal government becomes really rooted in our own self-sufficiency and our own ability to overcome obstacles.

Jaime Pinkham

considered as distinct, independent political communities, retaining their original natural rights as "the undisputed possessors of the soil from time immemorial . . ." (*Worcester* v. *Georgia*, 1832).

Although the number of such powers has been significantly reduced and some of these powers, while continuing to exist, have been weakened, Indian tribes still exercise their inherent governmental powers. Today, however, the federal government of the United States no longer recognizes Indian tribes as having the power to engage in war or the power to enter into treaties. In addition, while other tribal powers (such as criminal jurisdiction) still exist, they do so to a diminished degree when compared to the extent of their existence in previous, fully sovereign governments. What is more, no Indian tribe today exercises control over territory to the same extent it did 300 years ago.

Regardless, Indian tribes today retain all the governmental powers of any sovereign nation except as those tribal powers have been limited or eliminated by relinquishment or surrender by the tribe, a clear and express act of Congress, or being declared inconsistent with the tribe's dependent status.

There are three different ways in which sovereign tribal powers have been reduced over the years.

First, historically speaking, Indian tribes have voluntarily surrendered some of their sovereign powers. Usually, this reduction occurred in the process of entering into treaties with the United States. Treaties were devices designed to secure peace and obtain land for colonization and settlement. Tribes typically surrendered vast amounts of their original territory by treaties, and they typically agreed to move to reservations. Other sovereign powers were also frequently surrendered in the process. For example, many tribes agreed to turn white men who committed crimes against Indians over to the Indian agent rather than deal with the criminals themselves.

Second, tribal powers have been limited by clear and express acts of Congress. The Supreme Court has ruled that Congress has plenary (or total) power over Indian affairs. In other words, Congress can abrogate (or take away) treaty-reserved rights, change a tribe's jurisdiction, or even take away tribal land. The only limitations on these congressional powers are that

⋀ if it is to be legal, the law must clearly and expressly indicate that it is taking a tribal right—it cannot be done by implication— and

⋀ if the right taken is a property right, Congress must provide just compensation.

Third, tribal powers have sometimes been deemed inconsistent with a tribe's dependent status. Such declarations are typically made by federal courts whenever a particular sovereign power is inconsistent with the relationship the tribe now has with the United States. The sovereign power to wage war, for example, would be inconsistent with a tribe's status because the United States is the trustee or protector of the tribe and it, not the tribe, maintains military forces to protect the tribe and the nation.

> "Their relationship to the United States resembles that of a ward to his guardian."

Through these legal machinations, Indian tribes have come to be called "quasi-sovereigns," "limited sovereigns," and "semi-sovereigns" by federal courts in their analyses of tribal powers. The powers that tribes exercise today are nevertheless the same inherent sovereign powers they possessed and exercised centuries ago. We must and do recognize, however, that some of these powers exist in altered form and that others have been totally extinguished or reduced over the years.

NEZ PERCE SOVEREIGNTY

Like other Indian tribes, the Nez Perce Tribe originally possessed every attribute of a sovereign government. Although the aboriginal Nez Perce Tribe exercised its full range of governmental powers, its form of government and the forms of governmental activities were different from those forms common today. Indian tribes have been recognized as distinct, independent political communities (*Worcester v. Georgia*, 1832) and domestic dependent nations (*Cherokee Nation v. Georgia*, 1831). The courts have also recognized that those powers that are lawfully vested in an Indian tribe are not, in general, delegated powers granted by express acts of Congress. They are, rather, the inherent powers of a limited sovereign that have never been extinguished.

That the Nez Perce Tribe was viewed as a sovereign entity by the United States was confirmed by the fact that the United States negotiated treaties with the Tribe in 1855, 1863, and 1868 (Appendices 2-4). Treaties, by definition, are agreements between sovereign governments. Indian treaties are accorded the same dignity as treaties with foreign nations (*United States v. 43 Gallons of Whiskey*, 1876). The primary effect of these treaties was the cession by the Tribe to the United States of millions of acres of tribal land, typically resulting in the creation of the reservation boundaries. The Nez Perce Tribe, for example, reserved certain rights to pasture livestock on open and unclaimed lands and to take fish at all "usual and accustomed" places inside and *outside* the reservation boundaries.

"Its trust responsibility imposes an independent obligation upon the federal government to remain loyal to the Indians and to advance their interests."

In addition to rights expressly reserved by these treaties, established case law recognizes that the Nez Perce Tribe reserved whatever tribal rights existed at the time that were not specifically conveyed away. Contrary to many popular myths and opinions about the effect of Indian treaties, the United States Supreme Court has held that "the treaty was not a grant of rights to the Indians, but a grant of rights from them—a reservation of those not granted" (*United States v. Winans*, 1905).

Federal Trust Responsibility

The concept of "trust responsibility" was first announced in a U.S. Supreme Court decision written by Chief Justice John Marshall. In *Cherokee Nation v. Georgia* 1831, Marshall stated that rather than being deemed "foreign nations" that tribes "may, more correctly, perhaps, be denominated domestic dependent nations. . . in a state of pupilage. Their relationship to the United States resembles that of a ward to his guardian."

The United States has a trust responsibility to Indian tribes that guides and limits the federal government in dealings with tribal governments. The treaties confirmed that the United States government has a fiduciary trust responsibility to insure that land uses in the ceded areas and in the tribe's usual and accustomed areas continue to be maintained in a manner consistent with the treaties. The trust obligations of the United States extend to all federal agencies and to all federal actions, and the implementation of federal statutory schemes affecting Indian people, Indian land, and Indian resources, must be judged by the most exacting fiduciary standard. Consequently, the federal government and its implementing agencies are obligated to use their expertise and authority in meaningful consultation with the tribes in order to safeguard natural resources that are of crucial importance to tribal self-government and to tribal prosperity.

Its trust responsibility imposes an independent obligation upon the federal government to remain loyal to the Indians and to advance their interests. The purpose behind the trust doctrine is (and always has been) to insure the survival and welfare of Indian tribes and Indian people. As a result of the trust relationship, the federal government protects the tribes from interference and intrusion by state governments and state citizens.

The federal trust responsibility to the Indian tribes evolved from the 1886 landmark Supreme Court decision, *United States v. Kagama*, which found that the trust relationship between the federal government and the tribes conferred on Congress both the duty and the power to regulate tribal affairs.

In 1903, in *Lone Wolf v. Hitchcock*, the Supreme Court ruled that the trust relationship served as a source of power for Congress to take action on tribal land held under the terms of a treaty. The Supreme Court held that the status of the Indians who entered into the treaty and their relationship of dependency to the United States were such that Congress had a plenary power over the government's relations with the tribes.

In 1913, the Supreme Court ruled, in the *United States v. Sandoval*, that an unbroken line of federal, legislative, executive, and judicial actions had "attributed to the United States as a superior and civilized nation the power and the duty of exercising a fostering care and protection over all dependent Indian communities within its borders. . . ."

In cases involving the interpretation of Indian treaties or statutes, the Supreme Court has taken the position that the United States has intended to honor the treaties with the Indian tribes. This line of reasoning has led to the canons of construction related to Indian Law. Thus, *ambiguities in treaties are to be interpreted in favor of the Indians.* The treaties are to be interpreted as the Indians would have understood them at the time they were negotiated. Any abrogation of Indian rights is not implied but must be unequivocally stated.

First, a treaty is a treaty. It is a document between two sovereigns, country to country. I know what a sovereign can do. We can do a lot of things as a sovereign government, but we don't [do some things] because we want to work together with people. There is a lot you can do when you're sovereign.

Del White

Federal policies have affected our traditional, cultural, and ceremonial ways of life since they were created. Our "usual and accustomed" gathering places are now on private property, and access is very limited. We are challenged daily in protecting these retained rights.

Simone Wilson

With our treaty, the only thing that has changed is the battlefield, which is now the courts.

Anthony Johnson

To me, federal trust responsibility means that the federal government has specific responsibility to protect the rights of the Nez Perce people and that those rights are sacred areas for the Nez Perce people.

Arthur Taylor Jr.

My vision for the future, (hopefully in the year 3000), is that we are still a culturally distinct and separate people because that's what our people fought and died for. They did that. They said for us to be culturally distinct people because we were here before the U.S. Constitution.

Del White

For example, the right of the northwest tribes to one half of the salmon available for harvest at the usual and accustomed fishing sites of the tribes is secured by the application of these canons of construction to treaty language. The Treaties of 1855 reserve the right of Indians to fish in common with citizens of the territory.

In the legal dispute arising from this fishing issue, the State of Washington argued that the "in common with language" implied that the tribes reserved no more than the right to fish under state management. The Supreme Court recognized that such an interpretation would have eliminated tribal fishing rights. The tribes did not need a treaty to subject themselves to the same fishing laws as everyone else. The canons of construction imply that, to the Indians, what was intended was an agreement to share the fish equally.

Nez Perce General Council meeting at Lapwai, Idaho in 1930. (Photo courtesy of Mae Taylor.)

Chapter 4

Expanded Western Settlement and Federal Treaties

Relocation Era (1776-1886)

Many old men of the Nez Perces still have medals of Jefferson, dated 1804, which these adventurers gave them. They are held as priceless relics, and are not obtainable. These souvenirs were the pledge of friendship from the infant Republic—now grown to giant proportions—to a distant and simple race of savages. Then, in the days of our weakness, we came here offering friendship to the natives, and they accepted it, and have kept their part of the agreement; they proudly boast that they never shed the white man's blood. If, after growing up to the position of a great power, this treaty of amity—none the less sacred because unwritten—is to be violated by the misconduct of white men, let it not be without an effort on the part of Government to avert it.

Dr. Maurey

I feel the treaties provide a sacred trust to this generation and future generations.

Jaime Pinkham

The first Continental Congress recognized the importance of Indian Affairs both within the U.S. Constitution and in some of its first official congressional acts. The Louisiana Purchase of 1803 recognized and affirmed that the agreements between Spain and the Indian tribes should be honored by the United States until such time as other suitable articles could be established. The Northwest Ordinance of 1787, ratified by the U.S. Congress in 1789, declared: "The utmost good faith shall always be observed toward the Indians; their land and property shall never be taken from them without their consent."

The First Congress passed a number of laws to protect Indians from non-Indians. In 1790 Congress required that persons who wished to trade with Indians first obtain a federal license. Congress also authorized the prosecution of non-Indians who committed certain crimes against Indians. Furthermore, these laws also prohibited non-Indians from obtaining Indian land without the consent of the United States. In 1793 Congress prohibited non-Indians from settling on Indian lands and exempted Indians from complying with state trade regulations. Unfortunately, few of these laws were ever enforced, particularly those laws that might have discouraged immigrants from moving westward or those that provided tribes any meaningful recourse for trespass or crimes committed against them. When President Jefferson in 1803 sent explorers Lewis and Clark to find a trade route to and through the Northwest, one of the goals of this party was to secure "peace and friendship" with western tribes.

During this era (1776-1886) there were also significant changes in social and economic structure that affected all the tribes. As we have already noted, exotic and devastating diseases wiped out entire villages. Moreover, the nature of Native American tribalism was one of great individuality, an individuality that permitted great freedoms but that also generally prevented inter-tribal unification. The sacred belief held in common among the tribes that no one could "own" the land worked against North American Indian governments during this period.

Oldest known photo of Chief Joesph circa 1877. (Photo courtesy of Nez Perce National Historical Park.)

Feuding between Indian nations increased as more lands were being colonized in the West. Changes in weapons technology created greater numbers of casualties among feuding tribes. Consequently, as tribes struggled desperately to adjust and adapt to the changes now rapidly impacting their lands and their lives, military power on the continent shifted in favor of the United States. In 1830, Congress passed the Indian Removal Act, which authorized the President to negotiate with eastern tribes for their relocation west of the Mississippi River. Many tribes, at first removed from their aboriginal lands to new "permanent" homes in the Midwest, were soon forced to relocate even farther west to the Oklahoma Indian Territory. During this era, the United States government broke its treaties with Indians almost as soon as the treaties were ratified.

"The western expansion policy of 'Manifest Destiny' resulted in the loss of Indian lives, Indian lands, and security for Indian nations across the United States and its territories."

The western expansion policy of "Manifest Destiny" resulted in the loss of Indian lives, Indian lands, and security for Indian nations across the United States and its territories. The discovery of gold in California in the 1850s and the ensuing gold fever (accompanied by the continued spread of exotic diseases, governmental wars, and forced removals) produced cultural genocide and holocaust, and, in some cases, total the extinction of particular bands and even whole Indian nations. The near mass extinction of the great buffalo herds, symbolized by such legendary western figures as Buffalo Bill, helped to create situations of starvation and famine for many plains tribes, and, in fact, was part of an official policy to starve tribes into submission. Too many treaties were made and broken and too many official and unofficial wars were fought to document here. Apparently nothing could deter the western expansion of immigrants, towns, and railroads, and the extraction of Indian resources. Nearly a century after Congress passed the Northwest Ordinance of 1787, which recognized the sovereignty of Indian tribes, Congress also passed a law that eliminated the practice of making treaties with Indian tribes. The federal government no longer recognized Indian tribes as independent nations. It now proposed to deal with tribes by passing statutes that, unlike the treaties, did not require tribal consent.

NEZ PERCE RELOCATION OR REMOVAL ERA

(1855-1893)

The Nez Perce relocation (or removal) era is defined as that period of time when the Tribe entered into treaties and agreements that permitted land cessions to federal government, thus making way for thousands of intruders. This historical period should not be confused with the *Relocation Era* of the 1960s and 1970s. The Nez Perce Removal Era includes the Treaty of 1855, the Treaty of 1863, the Treaty of 1868, and the 1893 Nez Perce Agreement.

TREATY OF 1855

During the 1850s the federal government entered into treaties with Indian tribes all across the United States, including many of the Columbia Basin Tribes. In June of 1855, representatives of the United States federal government met at Walla Walla, Washington, with leaders of the Umatilla, Yakama, and Nez Perce nations to negotiate. Many of the other smaller tribes in the region, such as the Cayuse, the Palouse, and the Walla Walla were considered by the federal government to be a part of the Nez Perce, Umatilla, or Yakama tribes.

The Tribe waited four years for ratification of the Treaty of 1855, and why? Not because they revolted. On the contrary, they adhered faithfully to their duty and fealty. Were they rewarded by being made an exception and their treaty ratified itself? No. They were punished like hostiles, and their treaty was not ratified until 1859. By mismanagement they have never seen but little fulfillment of it by agents of the Government, and to crown it all, their reservation two years ago was invaded by 15,000 miners in contempt of the treaty and of their sacred rights most solemnly guaranteed to them. Thus everything has been done which the fates could invent to tempt these faithful allies into revolt.

Benjamin Alvord, 1864 Memorial to Nez Perce, Starr Maxwell

Many of the older guys could quote the the entire treaty. Men like Harrison Lott, Sam Slickpoo, Joe Blackeagle all were very eloquent speakers.

Loretta Halfmoon

The discovery of gold on Nez Perce land prompted thousands of miners to ignore the reservation boundaries established in the Treaty of 1855. (Photo courtesy of Nez Perce National Historical Park.)

The representatives of the federal government who negotiated the treaty at the Walla Walla Treaty Council included a man named Isaac Stevens (the newly appointed Governor of the Washington Territory, a title that also carried with it the position of Superintendent of Indian Affairs) and Joel Palmer, Superintendent of Indian Affairs for the Oregon Territory. Stevens was also the leader of the most northerly of the four Pacific Railroad Survey groups that the War Department had dispatched to discover the most feasible route through the Rocky Mountains for a railroad to the Pacific. Stevens' goal was to acquire as much land as possible as cheaply as possible for future colonists and to discover the cheapest and most practicable railroad route. The representatives from the tribes included (for the Nez Perce) Lawyer, Joseph, U-usinmalicun, James, Timothy, Red Wolf, Spotted Eagle, Three Feathers, Jason, Jacob, Cow-pook, Is-coh-tim, Kay-kay-mass, Tei-peo-lanitsakum, Billy, Toh-tohmolewat, The Snipe, Bold Eagle, and, later, Chief Looking Glass; (for the Cayuse) The Young Chief, Steachus, Camaspelu; (for the Walla Wallas) PeoPeoMoxMox; (for the Yakamas) Kamiakin, Owhi, Skloom, Kowassayie, Si-aywas, Skinpah; and (for the Palouse) Kohlatoose.

> "Stevens was impressed by the show, but he failed to recognize the significance of the Nez Perce entrance."

I was at the signing of the 1855 Treaty. Governor Stevens promised many things. He said they would put up sawmills, cut lumber, put up blacksmith shops, furnish us with farms and schools, give us cows, domestic animals, and help us to live a more healthful life. Governor Stevens said that we would still have access to hunt and fish on the ceded land and the use of timber for camping purposes. After making these promises they have failed to carry them out.

George Amos, 1911 Memorial to Nez Perce, Starr Maxwell

Stevens and his escort of forty-seven soldiers arrived at Mill Creek in the Walla Walla Valley on May 21, 1855. Tents, a log storehouse and banquet hall, and council chambers were set up in anticipation of the council. On May 24 representatives of the Nez Perce Nation (numbering at least 2500 people) made their entrance. As the Nez Perce chiefs rode forward to be formally introduced to the governor, a thousand Nez Perce warriors, riding two abreast and mounted on fine horses, circled the flagpole. They put on a show of horsemanship and dancing that was spectacular. Stevens was impressed by the show, but he failed to recognize the significance of the Nez Perce entrance. Our Nez Perce ancestors were not only honoring him as an important person: they were also demonstrating that the Nez Perce are a strong and important people who expect to be treated as equals.

By the time the other tribes had arrived (including the Cayuse, Walla Wallas, Palouse, Yakama, and Umatillas) there were about 5000 Indians in attendance. The council officially began on May 29, five days after the Nez Perce arrival. Stevens began his proceedings with a speech telling the people what wonderful things he had done for the Indian people on the west side of the Cascades. He said he was there to help and to protect the Indians in our part of the country. "If we make a treaty with you," the Governor told us, "you can rely on all its provisions being carried out strictly." Palmer made his speeches the next day. It was not until June 2 when the council convened again that it was time for the chiefs to be heard. The prevailing sentiment was against Stevens' proposals. The session on June 2, 1855, ended tensely.

Talks resumed two days later on June 4. Stevens proposed two reservations that had previously been mapped out. Both of his proposed reservation sites had been carefully thought out, but Stevens intentionally neglected to tell the Indians that he had specifically selected lands for their reservations that no white man yet wanted, and, perhaps most importantly, he made no mention of his desire to secure land for the railroad. The majority of the tribal representatives, nevertheless, were displeased with these proposals and reacted coldly.

Stevens then proposed a new scheme that called for three reservations, a proposal much more agreeable to the tribal leaders. Nevertheless, their prevailing sentiment and desire was to hold another council in the near future so they could take time to think and reflect about the ramifications of the treaty proposal. Stevens, however, determined to press the issue. Most of the tribal representatives knew, of course, that the reservation system was inevitable and that they would eventually end up signing a treaty, which many of them did several days later on June 11, 1855.

Salmon fishing was a right Indians had retained, not a privilege granted to the conquering whites. A privilege can be regulated, but a right cannot be regulated.

David Sohappy

The U. S. Constitution (Article VI, the Supremacy Clause, under Article I, Section 8, the Commerce Clause) verifies the rights the tribe has always had. . . . The first step is to educate our own tribal members about the treaties. Under the U. S. Constitution there are at least four times that Indian tribes are specifically mentioned. And prior to that, we always had the inherent right to self government, which predated the U.S. Constitution.

Samuel N. Penney

May, 1855. Walla Walla Council. Governor Stevens with Indians.

Depiction of the Treaty of 1855 at Walla Walla. (Photo courtesy of Columbia River Inter-Tribal Fish Commission.)

I was present at the treaty in 1855. We were told that we would be furnished with many conveniences such as blacksmith shops, tinsmith shops, gun shops, hospitals, sawmills, lumber, houses, fencing, schools, and some money. These promises and obligations were not carried out on the part of the Government.

Jim Matt, 1911
Memorial to Nez Perce, Starr Maxwell

. . . . in the Treaties a lot of our leaders recognized that alcohol was very damaging. In the negotiations of the treaties, there was mention of this by some of the leaders.

Julia Davis

By signing this treaty, the Nez Perce Tribe gave by cession to the United States some 7.5 million acres of tribal land. The treaty also resulted in the creation of the 1855 reservation. Regardless, the treaty also stipulated that the Nez Perce reserved certain rights (including the right to hunt, to gather, and to pasture livestock on open and unclaimed land and, naturally, to take fish at all "usual and accustomed places" both inside *and* outside the reservation boundaries). The treaty also required the Tribe to officially recognize the federal government and attempted to impose upon the Nez Perce against our will an Office of Principal Chief, a requirement that was completely unacceptable to many Nez Perce bands. Still, Chief Lawyer of Kamiah, a Christian convert who was friendly with the whites, assumed the official title of Head Chief.

In addition to rights expressly reserved by treaty, established case law recognizes that the Nez Perce Tribe reserved whatever tribal rights existed at the time that were not specifically conveyed away in the treaty. Contrary to many popular myths about the effect of Indian treaties, the United States Supreme Court has held that "the treaty was not a grant of rights to the Indians, but a grant of rights from them, a reservation of those [rights] not granted."

Nez Perce Encampment at Lapwai, Idaho, in 1910. (Photo courtesy of Nez Perce National Historical Park.)

TREATY OF 1863

One of the provisions of the Treaty of 1855 guaranteed that the government of the United States would prevent the trespass and invasion of the Nez Perce Reservation by immigrants. Without permission from the Tribe, no outsider could live on the Reservation. The following quotations, for example, are taken directly from the minutes of the 1855 Treaty negotiations with Governor Stevens and Superintendent Palmer at Walla Walla, Washington. Read carefully the promise that Superintendent Palmer makes to Chief Looking Glass regarding the sanctity of the reservation boundaries:

LOOKING GLASS: I want to know if an Agent will stay up in my country?
PALMER: Certainly.
LOOKING GLASS: Will you mark the piece of country that I have marked and say the Agent shall keep the whites out?
PALMER: None will be permitted to go there but the Agent and the persons employed, without your consent.
LOOKING GLASS: It is not for nothing I am speaking to my chiefs, it is to talk straight, it is just as if I were to see the President and talk to him it would be straight. . . . You have said to me that the whites shall not go over that line, none shall go into that country and this you said and it is said: And you will show to the President what we have said.

Even before Congress could ratify the 1855 Treaty, mass trespass was already occurring on the Nez Perce reserved lands. In 1858, a miner by the name of Elias D. Pierce, after repeatedly lying about his intentions in order to trespass on Nez Perce land, discovered gold on the reservation. In the wake of gold fever, hundreds of other miners were soon ignoring the existence of the 1855 boundaries, committing mass trespass, and attempting to establish boomtowns like Orofino in various locations across the reservation. Steamboats from the coast made their way up the Snake and Clearwater rivers inside the 1855 treaty boundaries, bringing with them more immigrant trespassers and squatters, more diseases, more exotic plants, and, of course, "supplies" for the camps. The town of Lewiston was soon formed on Nez Perce reserved land at the confluence of the Snake and Clearwater rivers and served as a base camp for the miners. In other words, even Lewiston, later to become the first Idaho Territory capital, was established in clear viola-

At the time of the making of the Treaty of 1863 the privileges granted to us under the Treaty of 1855 were still in force—that is, that we still have the right to hunt and fish on any of the land formerly owned by the Nez Perces. At the present time, if a Nez Perce wished to hunt or fish, even near his own home, he must procure a game license before he is permitted to do so. Our people hold that in direct violation of their rights under the treaties and a confiscation of the principal part of the compensation they were to receive for their large cessions of land.

Henry E-nah-la-lamkt, 1911 Memorial to Nez Perce, Starr Maxwell

In 1863 a further cession of land was made, but our rights to the game, fish, etc. were still retained; finally in 1893, when we made the last cession of land, we were guaranteed all the treaty rights theretofore promised. We were not paid the full amounts promised to us in the treaties and agreements, and we were not protected in our hunting and fishing rights. Many of our people are unjustly and wrongfully treated.

Starr Maxwell, 1911 Memorial to Nez Perce, Starr Maxwell

tion of the 1855 Treaty. The promise of the United States government to protect the rights of the Nez Perce was irretrievably broken.

Naturally, tribal officials objected to and protested against these blatant violations of the 1855 Treaty and appealed to the federal government to keep its promises. Instead of keeping its word by honoring the Treaty, enforcing its terms, and preventing mass trespass (not to mention the outright theft of huge quantities of gold from the reservation), the United States government produced a new treaty on June 9, 1863. This proposed treaty drastically reduced the reservation's size from 7.5 million acres to 750,000 acres. The government also attempted to deny Nez Perce claims to lands in Oregon, Washington, and other parts of Idaho. Our Nez Perce leaders, however, continued to insist on the inclusion in the "new" treaty for provisions such as the right to hunt and fish at all usual and accustomed places as reserved under the 1855 Treaty. They also included a clause to reserve all springs and fountains, as well as perpetual right-of-way to use those springs and fountains as watering places.

True: this treaty was signed by the Nez Perce leaders who resided within the proposed boundaries of the new reservation, but it was absolutely and flatly denied and rejected by the leaders outside the boundaries of the proposed reservation. To their consternation, on June 9, 1863, Lawyer and fifty-one members of his group nevertheless signed the treaty. The government was able to secure the signatures of every headman whose lands the new treaty of 1863 would not affect. The government, however, never did secure the signatures of Joseph, White Bird, and other tribal leaders who lived inside the boundaries of the 1855 reservation but outside the proposed new reservation.

The government agents later boasted that they had been able to secure about 7 million acres of Nez Perce land in the new treaty at a cost that did not exceed eight cents per acre. Land that was lost in the 1863 Treaty included the Wallowa, Imnaha and Grande Ronde country, valleys in the Snake and Salmon rivers, Asotin, Camas Prairie, and trails to the Bitteroot Valley. To this day, many Nez Perce still refer to the Treaty of 1863 as the "Steal Treaty." It reduced the size of Nez Perce reserved lands by about 90%. The Nez Perce lands were now 10% of their size in 1855 Treaty. It took four years for the 1863 Treaty to be ratified by Congress. President Andrew Johnson signed it on April 20, 1867.

Needless to say, by 1867 the gold rush on the reservation had ended. Still, it was this brief gold boom that initiated the 1863 Treaty and changed the boundaries of the original reservation—and the lives of the Nez Perce people—forever.

In 1875 President Ulysses S. Grant established a commission to meet with the Joseph Band in Oregon to discuss their grievances. That commission found that the Joseph Band was not bound by the Treaty of 1863. The President then signed an Executive Order to establish for Joseph and his people a reservation near Wallowa, Oregon. Due to a mapping error, however, the reservation was established on lands occupied by white immigrants, and the Executive Order was rescinded. Soon, the same federal government that had failed to protect Nez Perces from citizen aggressions and mass trespass had dispatched military units to enforce the 1863 Treaty upon those Nez Perce bands that had refused to sign. One result was the outbreak of what is now known as the "Nez Perce War of 1877" or the "Joseph War."

"Said trees would, in a few years, have been a source of great wealth to the Indians."

In 1864, Idaho Territorial Governor Caleb Lyon wrote a letter of report to the Commissioner of Indian Affairs regarding the conditions of the Nez Perce Agency in Lapwai and conditions among the Nez Perce people in general. This report exposes the lie that the federal government was "taking care" of the Nez Perce in accordance with its treaty obligations. In that letter Governor Lyon states that he has been "busy…in examining the manner in which the powerful, yet always friendly Nez Perce Nation have been dealt with." He goes on at some length, however, as follows:

> 1st I find no schoolhouse, church or Indians under instruction.

> 2nd I find the little valley patches of land cultivated by the Indians fenced with brush of their own labor, while the papers [official records] show that the lumber sawed at the mill was used for that purpose.

> 3rd I find that logs have been purchased and paid for by those in charge of the Agency from the appropriations, and sawed at the Agency Mill, the Sawyer paid by the Government, and the lumber sold to white persons, and further that the saw mill has been of little or no value to the Indians.

Many of our people were killed in the Joseph War and many more died from the hardships they suffered from the removal to the Indian Territory and their return to the north. We feel that the Government now, at this late day, should carry out all these obligations to the few that remain of our people and should protect the individual in their personal rights and should pay us what is coming to us. They should also pay us for the loss of our game and fish, protect us against the seizure of parts of our allotments, give us full liberty as guaranteed, and instead of discouraging us in every way possible, they should encourage us and let us use our own free actions to help ourselves.

Yellow Bull, 1911 Memorial to Nez Perce, Starr Maxwell

When the agreement of 1863 was made, we were guaranteed all of our rights under the former treaties, which we understood to mean our hunting and fishing rights. We also understood it to mean the payment and fulfillment to us of all the moneys and obligations which was promised. Much of our trouble heretofore arose on account of the Government not carrying out its obligations to our people.

Benjamin Whitman, 1911 Memorial to Nez Perce, Starr Maxwell

4th I find that white men under the sanction of those in charge of the Agency, have been allowed to go onto, and cut and remove trees from the land owned by the Indians and for proof of the assertion, large rafts are now strung along the river, which are to be cut up for fuel, for supply of this Town, also for the steamers which run on Snake River. While most of the logs in said rafts are good saw logs — the same being worth for fuel from ten to fifteen dollars per cord.

5th I find that one of the nearest and most valuable groves of trees to the Agency, most of which were young and thrifty trees, have been cut down by white men and the wood sold to Government. Said trees would, in a few years, have been a source of wealth to the Indians.

6th I find that the [non-Indian] farmers at the Agency have lived on the United States, seemingly in indolence, not raising enough for their own sustenance, neither devoting any time to instructing the Indians, and although the land is very rich and fruitful, I must say [if] it might be possible to till it in a worse manner, I cannot believe it was ever done. With forty acres badly fenced and worse cultivated, with a superintendent of farming and two assistant farmers and two laborers, raising only 150 bushels of oats, 150 bu of wheat, 60 bu of corn and 400 bu of potatoes.

7th I find the wife of one of the employees set down on the [official record] papers as a Blacksmith and the wife of another employee to be an Assistant Teacher, who has never taught a single hour.

8th I find the name of a Physician on the papers at a salary of $1200 per annum who is not at the Agency more than 3 hours per week —who is and draws salary as Surgeon at Fort Lapwai. I find also that the Supt. of farming at the Agency, at a salary of $1200, drawing a salary of $500 per year, as interpreter at said military fort.

9th I found the building at the Agency formerly used as a sutlers store had been sold to Robert Newell who afterwards swapped the same with Supt. Wallace for the building erected for a school house.

(No 10th)

11th I find the one good building at the Agency to be the Mill, which mill has never been given exclusively for use of the Nez Perces.

12th I find nothing but criminal negligence and indifference to the Treaty Stipulations with the Indians by a majority of those at the Agency.

13th I have found great discontent among the Indians owing to such state of affairs. . . .

We feel that we have not been protected in the rights granted us under the treaties, especially the rights to hunt and fish and use the streams, springs, and fountains, the roads and rivers on the ceded lands. None of our people have the right today to hunt and fish without procuring a license; even then their privileges are limited. I, myself was arrested three years ago for killing a deer and fined $90. Our people believe that we have the right to the game and fish anywhere within the boundaries of the 15,000,000 acres we originally owned. We have never given up those rights; they have been taken from us without our consent and without our advice.

*Black Eagle, 1911
Memorial to Nez Perce, Starr Maxwell*

The treaties entered into with this government to help us, to take care of us, and the government made promises which I think they should keep.

Gladys Allen

Noted Chiefs. (Photo courtesy of Nez Perce National Historical Park.)

14th I find there is neither a gunsmith nor wagon makers or tin shop on the reserve.... I think changes are absolutely necessary for the well being of the Service and Offices should not be filled until buildings are erected, and fences made and land tilled so as to render this Agency a semi self supporting establishment.

This report is perhaps one of the most revealing official documents verifying the failure of the federal government to live up to its treaty promises. It is, however, only one of many by various writers.

TREATY OF 1868

The 1868 Treaty, essentially an amendment to the Treaty of 1863, granted the federal government land at Lapwai for a military reservation and compensated the Tribe with more promises: to replace Indian school funds that had previously been stolen, to protect the timber on the reservation, and to provide additional twenty-acre lots off the reservation if the reserve did not prove large enough to supply enough good agricultural land for all the Indians. The 1863 Treaty also provided for the plowing and fencing of Nez Perce allotments and the removal of Indians to the reservation. After the ratification of this treaty, Congress finally appropriated funds so that schools could at last be opened.

Chief Joseph Council 1880. (Photo courtesy of Nez Perce National Historical Park.)

NEZ PERCE WAR OF 1877:

A RESULT OF THE RELOCATION OR REMOVAL ERA

Although mislabeled the "Nez Perce War" or the "Joseph War," the Nez Perce did not start, nor did they desire, this famous conflict. In 1877, seventy-two years after the arrival of the peace-seeking Lewis and Clark Expedition, at least fifty Nez Perces had been murdered and their murderers left unpunished. As our resources—including gold, land, water, and timber—continued to disappear, the government continued to propose new treaties to prevent us from seeking redress for empty and broken promises. The Gold Rush of the 1860s brought over 50,000 gold miners onto the reservation within a five-year period. The federal government sought to justify its apathy and inaction by diminishing the newly formed reservation to a tenth of its size. This agreement, the Treaty of 1863, which was intended to legalize what were clearly illegal acts by trespassers, was never signed, however, by the majority of the landowners who were represented by the chiefs of the respective bands.

Finally in 1877, the federal government, acting on the demands of the white immigrants, dispatched U.S. military forces under the primary leadership of General Howard. Breaking every agreement it had made with the Nez Perce, the military demanded that all the bands outside

As we drove across the country to Lake Waha, I pointed out the boundary lines as was last established, but these lines were not in accordance with the first survey. It seems that some white man had settled on the west boundary line before this treaty was made. By theses erroneous lines we lost 2,000 acres of land which should have been included in the estimates of the lands we sold in 1893.

Philip McFarland, 1911 Memorial to Nez Perce, Starr Maxwell

Chief Joseph was a strong man. He was clever. He led the Nez Perce to many victories, but he didn't win with muscle. He beat them with his heart and mind.

Solo Greene

Many of our people had been killed by white men on our reservation. But at no time was anything done to punish them. The discovery of gold on our reservation brought thousands of white men. That was the beginning of our trouble. Those white killers were never bothered from living on our lands. They were still there. Still robbing and shooting or hanging Indians.

Yellow Wolf

A treaty is a contract between sovereign nations. States do not have the authority to enter into a treaty. The purpose of the treaties with the Indian nations was not to give rights but to take them away.

Samuel N. Penney

Treaties are the law of the land, but the essence of our existence is the uniqueness of who we are as Nimiipuu. *Those aspects that define us are tribal, individual and familial. These aspects include but are not restricted to our language, cultural values, customs, ceremonies, rights of passage, history, heritage, hunting, fishing and gathering. All these aspects are the issues that we as a tribe must protect and maintain for future generations.*

Simone Wilson

of the 1863 boundaries move onto the reservation within thirty days (This incident, however, marks only one of countless shameful military acts committed against Indian people in the 1800s). Under great duress, these free Nez Perce bands met for one last time near present day Tolo Lake before intending to move onto the reservation. The inequity, injustice, and absolute absurdity of this forced move from their beloved and rightful homeland tempted three Nez Perce youths to avenge the deaths of their father and uncle. They took very specific and limited revenge on a total of seventeen white immigrants along the Salmon River.

Knowing that an "unjust" government prevented them from retaliating in this manner, the chiefs sought council and met at Chief White Bird's village near the present day town of the same name. In the meantime, when General Howard heard of the attacks, he sent Colonel Perry, ninety-nine cavalrymen, and eleven volunteers to investigate the rumors. They arrived at dawn, June 17, 1877. Ignoring the white flag of truce produced by Nez Perce warriors, Perry and his forces raised their standard and launched an all-out attack, hoping to make a quick end of it. The federal military lost sixty-seven soldiers in the ensuing battle while only two members of Nez Perce nation were wounded.

Realizing they could now never make amends with the army, the non-treaty Nez Perce then began an 1100-mile journey of retreat from the federal troops. After a series of battles and skirmishes, the weary bands camped near the Bears Paw Mountains, only forty miles from the Canadian border they intended to cross in order to seek refuge and political asylum. Of the nearly 800 Nez Perce people who left the Idaho Territory, only 431 survived. Chief White Bird managed to escape with about half of those, while Chief Joseph surrendered after being solemnly promised he could return to his homeland in the Wallowas.

After eight long years of exile and captivity in Indian Territory in Oklahoma, where all of the young died, the Nez Perce were finally freed. About half of the Nez Perce prisoners returned to the reservation in Idaho, while Chief Joseph and the rest took Chief Moses up on his offer to live with him and his people on the Colville Reservation in Nespelem, Washington. Other Nez Perce people were able to live on the Umatilla reservation with relatives. To protect themselves and their families wherever they found refuge, many of the surviving Nez Perce War veterans changed their names.

Through death and even intertribal disputes, this war divided our families: brothers from cousins, sisters from sisters, grandfathers and grandmothers from grandchildren, husbands from wives, aunts from nieces, uncles from nephews, fathers from sons, mothers from daughters. . . . Today we seek healing by acknowledging all of those who suffered and died to protect the peace and freedom of our coming generations.

WAR MEMORIALS

Each year the Nez Perce Tribe commemorates three of the significant battles that we fought in the 1877 War. We set aside these days on the calendar as Nez Perce War Memorials. Tribal members have the opportunity to visit the places where the armed conflicts took place and to remember through word and ceremony the sacrifices our ancestors made with their lives. The three war memorials include Whitebird (on June 17), Big Hole (on August 9), and Bears Paw (on October 5).

It is the way we honor our people that have passed on. That was my reason. That is the same reason that I try to keep the Seven Drum religion alive. Most of the people that were in the War of 1877 were not Christian people. They were non-treaty Indians that wanted to hang onto the old ways of the Indian culture: traditions and spirituality. If you make up your mind, you can do a lot of things. I just decided that I was going to do what my great-grandfather did. He decided for this purpose at the Bears Paw Battlefield. I guess I could say now that he was my role model, even though I didn't get to know him.

Horace Axtell

Front to back: Amy Carson and Audra Holt at the Whitebird Memorial. (Photo courtesy of Antonio Smith.)

CHAPTER 5

ALLOTMENT ERA

ALLOTMENT ERA (1887-1930)

The Alliance would have you believe that the Indians have few rights based on the Allotment. Non-Indians need to understand that we do still have treaty rights to protect us. The Alliance doesn't want us to have any say about what happens on the reservation. They think that the reservation is something government should do away with, but it is something which is supposed to be forever.

Gladys Allen

The allotment era is marked by the enthusiastic zeal of Christian and eastern philanthropic influences, both of which purported to be sympathetic to the plight of the great "red man" but both of which were nevertheless essentially patriarchal and culturally arrogant in their attitude of knowing "what was best" for us. These people fervently wanted the Indian people on reservations to adopt non-Indian ways. They encouraged this process by developing a system for individual ownership of lands, and in 1887 Congress passed the Dawes Allotment Act, ostensibly to teach Indians how to farm using European methods but also by providing individual Indians with an allotment of land.

The General Allotment Act was sponsored by Senator Henry Dawes and signed into law by President Grover Cleveland in 1887. The law was passed as a result of criticism to the reservation system and was yet another attempt to force cultural integration. The law had three main features.

The General Allotment Act forced Indian people to participate in the program or risk denial of previously guaranteed treaty rights and benefits. Allotment procedures preceded enrollment and legal recognition of tribal membership. The program further strained Nez Perce tribal unity, already troubled by religious and band allegiance problems.

Diane Mallickan

▲ First, every Indian in the United States would receive title to a piece of land. The stated intention was to provide every native family with a working farm. Heads of households received 160 acres, unmarried adults 80 acres, and children 40 acres.

▲ Second, since the reservations contained more land than would be "needed" because there was more than enough land for Indian allotment, the United States government would purchase those lands the tribes were willing to sell for purposes of further white colonization.

▲ Third, every tribal member who received an allotment would eventually become an American citizen. Special agents were appointed by the President to apportion reservation lands throughout the United States.

It was not, of course, until 1924 (37 years later) that full citizenship with voting rights was ever granted to any Indian irrespective of allotment issues. (Women's suffrage was declared constitutional two years earlier, in 1922, by the Nineteenth Amendment.)

Agnes Moses gathering fire wood. (Photo courtesy of Nez Perce National Historical Park.)

I am a Nez Perce Indian and a member of the tribal council. I served three years in the U.S. army. I know my people are loyal to the U.S. government, patriotic, law abiding citizens, and should be encouraged to continue to be such, but many things have occurred to discourage them, such as classification of our people, the withholding of their money, and the lack of consideration our people receive from the officials of the government when they make complaint thereof. Our people have lived up to all the treaties and agreements as they understand them, but the government has not lived up to the treaties and agreements and have misled us in the meaning of them.

*Homer Allen, 1911
Memorial to Nez Perce, Starr
Maxwell*

Section 6 of the General Allotment Act (Dawes Act) granted citizenship only to allottees upon issuance of trust patents and only to any Indian "who had voluntarily taken up ... his residence separate and apart from any tribe of Indians ... and [who] has adopted the habits of civilized life." Even in its language, the act is exclusionary, sexist, and culturally discriminatory.

THE NEZ PERCE ALLOTMENT ERA (1889-1930)

The Nez Perce allotment was carried out under the direction of Alice Fletcher, a federal agent sent West by the Commissioner of Indian Affairs in 1889. Her companion, E. Jane Gay, described Fletcher's effort this way:

> We were to convince them [the Nez Perce], man, woman, and child, of the desirableness of breaking their tribal relations... [in exchange] for American citizenship and a very moderately sized farm cut out of their tribal inheritance....The Indians notice that she [Alice Fletcher] makes no promises—they are sick of promises. She tells them... that they may stand up beside the white man in equality before the law. This is hard to grasp. The prospect of standing beside the white man is not a very brilliant one. The unadulterated Indian looks down upon the species of the white man.

Fletcher's work on the Nez Perce Reservation ended in 1894. Even the Nez Perce who had been granted land under the direction of Alice Fletcher, however, did not become official citizens until 1924.

Farming in the valley near Lapwai in the early 1900s. (Photo courtesy of Nez Perce National Historical Park.)

NEZ PERCE AGREEMENT 1893

Pressure from the Dawes Act led to the Nez Perce Agreement of 1893. Although some people view the agreement as a treaty, the negotiation process was different from the negotiating processes of the previous two treaties. In December of 1892, the Nez Perce organized a council for the purpose of discussing the allotment process and to redress grievances against the government. Among the grievances the tribe sought to address were outstanding claims by Nez Perce Indians who had served the U.S. Army as scouts during the War of 1877 but who had never been compensated for their services as promised. The Nez Perce sought

- ▲ to prohibit liquor on the reservation
- ▲ to ensure that church lands remained under tribal control
- ▲ and also to ensure that any agreement regarding the allotment of Nez Perce lands include what is known as a Savings Clause.

This clause would reiterate once more that (with the exceptions of those changes specifically stated) the rights of the Tribe would remain intact as in the original treaty with the U.S. government.

The council representatives on behalf of the Nez Perce Tribe were Reverend Archie Lawyer, James Lawyer, Reverend William Wheeler, Reverend James Hines Bartholomew, and James Reuben. The U.S. representatives included Perrin Whitman (interpreter), W.D. Robbins (Indian agent), Cyrus Beede (Chairman of the Commission), Albert Schleiker (Lewiston merchant), and James Allen (on leave from Commission of Indian Affairs Office from Washington D.C.).

James Reuben insisted that everything said be recorded in writing. The Commission recorded the first meeting but inexplicably failed to record the negotiations beyond that point. During the first council, the tribal representatives were strongly opposed to the opening of the reservation to non-Indians. The Nez Perce purported to have a willing buyer for tribal lands: a railroad capitalist who would pay more than what the government offered. The idea of selling to a higher bidder, however, was rejected based on the U.S. Supreme Court cases *Johnson v. McIntosh* (1823), which held that only the United States can negotiate with tribes for the purchase of title to lands.

The tribal representatives voiced their complaints on a variety of matters including their opposition to the allotment of the reservation. As a

I was here when the Agreement of 1893 was made. At the time of the signing of this agreement most of the people had been allotted lands, but quite a number who were living and entitled to allotments had not received land. After the agreement more than 100 allotments were canceled. Many people today have no allotments. We believe that every Nez Perce living between 1891 and August 1894 was entitled to and should have received allotments.

*George Amos, 1911
Memorial to Nez Perce, Starr Maxwell*

I was present at the signing of the agreement of 1893. My understanding was that we were selling only the surplus land and that it was estimated at 542,275 acres. Since this cession has been made many allotments have been cancelled that were not included in the sale and was no part of the 542,275 acres. We believe that the allotments—something over 110—that have been cancelled should revert to the tribe, or that the true value thereof should be paid to the people in the amount of $3 per acre which we received for the surplus land.

Harrison Red Wolf, 1911 Memorial to Nez Perce, Starr Maxwell

result, the Commissioners added clauses to the model agreement they brought to the negotiation. Most importantly, the requested "savings clause" was added. The savings clause states, "The existing provisions of all former treaties with said Nez Perce Indians not consistent with the provisions of this agreement are hereby continued in full force and effect."

After three negotiation sessions when the tribal leaders still refused to sell, however, the federal Commissioners adopted a new and even more effective strategy: they held smaller and smaller meetings. Outside of these small formal meetings, the commissioners traveled around the reservation to gather signatures from male members of the Tribe who could be somehow convinced to sign the agreement outside the council format. Within six months, a "majority" of the men had purportedly signed the agreement, and the commission returned it to the Secretary of the Interior.

Although the Tribe raised questions about the Commission's tactics, an investigation conducted by the federal government found no irregularities.

This 1893 agreement included other articles regarding sawmills on the reservation, a process for opening land to settlement, the use of lands for religious purposes, allotments to deceased tribal members, and per capita payments.

Land Distribution

Of the 140 million acres set aside as Indian lands in 1887 in the United States, only 50 million remained in Indian ownership by 1934. At that time the allotment system was abolished as a total failure in making farmers of Indians. It was, nevertheless, a resounding success in opening up reservation lands to white people after the treaty makers had promised Indians their reservations would remain intact.

The allotment system arguably produced even greater poverty on the reservation than the relocation era. Individual tribal members who attempted to farm were left to deal with unscrupulous Indian agents who secured rent from white farmers to lease Indian ground. Tribal farmers did not receive fair market prices for either their produce or their livestock. Furthermore, payments for lands sold were held up in Congress for many, many years. Both the Treaty Era and Allotment

Era bear witness to countless atrocities perpetrated against Indians. Criminal offenses against tribal members went unpunished, monies allocated for the sale of lands took years to reach the Indian sellers, rations were "lost" or spoiled, favoritism by unscrupulous agents created greater division and hostility within the Tribe, and medical supplies and medical assistance promised in the treaties were never delivered. This era marked the most significant changes for tribes: from nations of prosperity to reservations of despair.

Although the sale from the "surplus" lands brought a few years of short-term prosperity, the long-term effects of the allotment were disastrous. By 1902 thirteen towns and twenty post offices had been established on the Nez Perce Reservation. Bootlegging became a common crime, and the law against it was not enforced. The arrival of commercial agriculture made the traditional life styles of the Nez Perce appear anachronistic and obsolete. Worse: the arrival of commercial agriculture had devastating cultural impacts. Diseases (including infectious diseases like tuberculosis) became even more common. With less native food available (fewer camas and other healthy roots, fewer salmon, fewer elk, fewer buffalo, fewer eels,) dietary diseases became much more prevalent.

Because of the Allotment Act, only about eleven percent of the Nez Perce Reservation today is still owned by tribal members. As a result, parcels of tribal land (generally rectangular in shape) are separated by parcels

Receiving payments from BIA in 1895. Left to Right: Fred Bremmer (Kendrick Bank rep), Three Feathers (Me-tot-we-tes), Howard J. Howe, Redhorn (Taawis-ilp'ilp), James Edward Conner, Howard J. Howe (Lewiston National Bank rep). (Photo courtesy of Nez Perce National Historical Park.)

of land owned by non-Indians. Consequently, the Nez Perce Indian Reservation, with its alternating Indian and non-Indian owned land sections, is sometimes referred to as a "checkerboard reservation."

CLASSIFICATION SYSTEM

Nez Perce Reservation. Gray squares represent land that is owned by tribal members. (Illustration courtesy of Nez Perce Land Services.)

It was during the Allotment Era (1887-1930) that the Nez Perce people were victimized by an "official" classification system that penalized them for retaining traditional religious beliefs and culturally appropriate behavior. The information on the classification system given below was taken from the *Memorial of the Nez Perce Indians* compiled by Starr J. Maxwell. Individuals were assigned a classification based on brief interviews with the agent or the agent's assessment of personal reputations. The classification system outlined in Starr Maxwell's *Memorial of the Nez Perce Indians* in 1911 functioned on a three-tiered system:

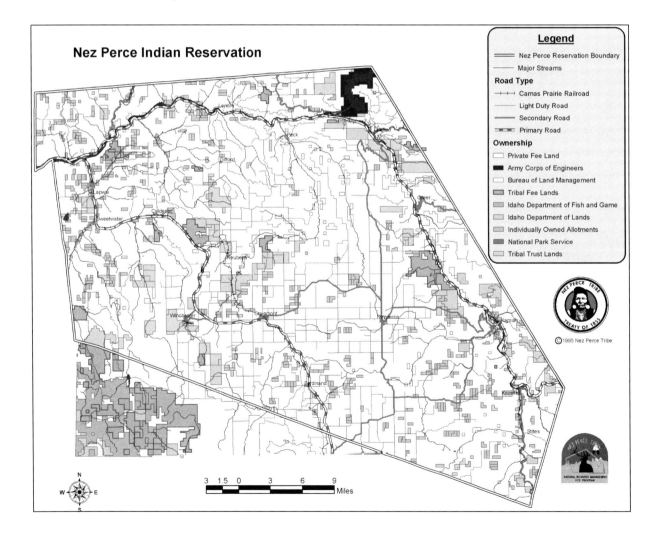

Class 1 people appeared comfortably assimilated into Euro-American ways. "Classification 1" generally implied church membership, willingness to send children to boarding schools, and successful farming habits. Class 1 people were permitted to manage their own financial resources without government interference. That is, they could receive their lease payments directly, decide how to manage their per capita payments, their farm or business income, and they could establish credit accounts with local merchants.

Class 2 people had limited control of financial and land resources.

Class 3 people (generally those most reluctant to abandon traditional cultural lifestyles or those who maintained lifestyles that agents found antithetical to "civilization") were categorized as incompetent. The agent administered income for Class 3 Nez Perce people and released funds to them when (and only if) circumstances suited him. He also controlled their lease arrangements and demanded that lease money belonging to Class 3 Nez Perce be presented to him rather than the Nez Perce property owner. The agent refused to respond to Nez Perce requests for financial statements or to provide information on the status of an individual's banking account.

The Allotment Era also marked the establishment of boarding schools both on and off the reservations. Indian children as young as five years old were shipped away to schools far from their homes where they were required to speak English. In some schools, including the Carlisle Indian School in Pennsylvania, students from different tribes boarded together, frequently resulting in their complete isolation and alienation from family, culture, and familiar surroundings. Many Nez Perce children from Idaho and Washington ended up in schools in Utah and Oregon. The schools were charged with the responsibility of teaching the children domestic skills: sewing, cooking, cleaning, and some vocational skills such as typing (for the girls) and agriculture (for the boys). Teachers frequently punished the children for speaking their native languages and practicing their native religions and cultural ways. Often, children ended up much like indentured servants. Few, if any, ever returned home without deep emotional scars. Some never returned.

CHAPTER 6

SHIFTING WINDS OF MODERN FEDERAL INDIAN POLICY

INDIAN REORGANIZATION ERA (1934-1960)

I've read the treaties. They are very clear in what they say: We will give them this land, and we will treat them as sovereign nations, and we will make provisions for their health and education. Those treaties were written in exchange for a significant portion of America.

Senator John McCain
Arizona Republic, 1977

In the early 1930s federal Indian policy changed abrubtly. A number of factors, including the dismal failure of the Allotment Act, the onset of the Great Depression that restricted the amount of funds available to whites for land purchase, and the public criticism of federal Indian policy, resulted in change. President Franklin D. Roosevelt signed the Indian Reorganization Act in 1934. The Act contained four major stipulations:

1. It recognized tribal governments and their inherent sovereign powers.
2. It made federal funds available for tribes to purchase additional lands.
3. It set up a loan program for tribal governmental operations.
4. It established programs to assist in the economic development of Indian tribes.

John Collier, who had been involved in the Indian policy reform movement, was appointed by President Roosevelt as Commissioner of Indian Affairs.

Commissioner Collier declared that "No interference with Indian religious life or expression will be tolerated. The cultural history of Indians is in all respects to be considered equal to that of any non-Indian group." This declaration and other declarations of national policy, however, along with changes to the law, were slow to be realized and felt, however, on reservations in the West. Even so, these declarations and changes were nevertheless truly significant for recognizing the inherent rights of tribes to govern themselves, for allocating funds to uphold the promises of the treaties, and for assistance in the development of tribal resources.

From 1935 to 1953 Indian land holdings increased by 2 million acres and federal funds were spent on tribal medical facilities, tribal irrigation works, tribal roads, tribal homes, and tribal community schools. The advent of World War II diverted public and government attention

Richard Halfmoon, Nez Perce Tribe Executive Committee Chairman 1955-1965.
(Photo courtesy of Nez Perce National Historical Park.)

away from economic well being of the tribes, however, and the tribal reservation system declined. It is nevertheless significant to note that even though the relationship between the tribes and the federal government has always been marked by gross injustice to Indians, Indian men and Indian women have always enlisted in the Armed Services to defend the United States. In fact, over the entire course of U.S. military history, Indians have a higher rate of enlistment in the Armed Services on a per capita basis than any other majority or minority group.

NEZ PERCE REORGANIZATION ERA (1934-1953)

Although the Indian Reorganization Act benefited many tribes across North America, the Nez Perce Tribe rejected it.

Allen Slickpoo, speaking to a history class at the University of Idaho in 1995, stated that

> The Tribe based its decision at that time upon information it received from Archie Phinney, a Nez Perce anthropologist who had studied in Leningrad, Russia, and at Columbia University. The goal of Phinney was to have the Tribe write their own constitution and by-laws, shape their own future, and have true sovereignty. The present form of government that is practiced by the Tribe today, with nine council members, was formed during that time.

Many of the tribal members who were active in the formulation of this plan had already been living independently, adjusting to reservation life, and trying to cope with a cash economy. These were Nez Perce who, in addition to their own hunting and gathering activities, also had huge gardens, some as large as several acres. Out of this time came the reservation garden clubs and other organizations who managed to adapt quickly to the different political system. These organizations and the people in them took an active part in supporting a tribal council that could speak and fight for them.

Nez Perce tribal member Allen Pinkham painted the following picture of that time period:

> Creating our own form of government was good, but it meant giving up some forms of traditional tribal govern-

ment and doing business in the old ways. The old 'Chief's System' was seemingly of the past, but there are certainly many forms of it in today's tribal system. Nonetheless, it was a time of tribes gaining control of their own affairs and their own business as well as a time for satisfying the U.S. government. The main point was to solve [the problem of] how tribes could best govern their people and maintain tribal sovereignty.

TERMINATION ERA (1953-1970)

This era marked another abrupt change in what can only be described as a schizophrenic federal Indian policy. Now the federal government sought to end the unique federal/ tribal relationship by dissolving recognition of treaty rights and reservation boundaries, as well as dividing tribal members' holdings and assets acquired by tribal governments. The Termination Era is marked by a national political effort to assert state rights over the rights of tribes. State governments had long resented the notion of tribal sovereignty and sought to gain control of tribal resources and tribal affairs.

In 1953 Congress officially adopted the termination policy under House Concurrent Resolution 108, which was designed to "free" Indians from

Congressman Gorton's legislative agenda suggests that Indians are enjoying some special rights based on race. But Indian sovereignty has nothing to do with race. It is a political status that defines the relationship of the tribes to the federal government.... Tribal nations have kept up their end of treaty agreements made with the United States. Now they look to the federal government to start doing the same. If there is a deep distrust among Indian nations toward the federal government, it's because ill-informed politicians like Senator Gorton scheme to keep us down.

Mark Anthony Rol (Bad River Ojibway) Seattle Times,1997

Nez Perce (Elizabeth Wilson and William Parsons) drying salmon in 1966 at Craigmont, Idaho. (Photo courtesy of Nez Perce National Historical Park.)

The Congress shall have the power to . . . regulate commerce with foreign nations, and among the several states, and with the Indian tribes;

US Constitution Article 1, Section 8, Clause 3

After World War II, the veterans' attitudes changed the ways many Indian people thought. In 1948 they revised the tribal constitution, making it one of the strongest. The veterans wanted a voice in tribal government, but the Bureau of Indian Affairs was reluctant. Politicians pointed out that the veterans served this country and died for this country, so that created a strong voice.

Allen Slickpoo Sr.

federal control and grant them full citizenship rights. In an effort to further reduce federal responsibilities to tribes, Congress passed Public Law 280, which conveyed to designated states full criminal and limited civil jurisdiction over Indian reservations and consented to the assumption of such jurisdiction by any additional states who sought to assume it. The idea was purportedly to improve police protection for Indians, but, of course, it had the opposite effect for many tribes.

Many states sought to abrogate treaty-reserved rights of hunting, fishing, and gathering and protection and prosecution of crimes committed against Indian people or on Indian lands.

In 1968 Public Law 280 was changed to require the consent of Indian tribes before states could assume jurisdiction. Many tribes fought feverishly to rescind the termination policies. This effort led to the building of national tribal coalitions including the formation of the National Congress of American Indians and the National Tribal Chairmen's Association.

NEZ PERCE TERMINATION ERA (1953-1970)

Not since the onslaught of U.S. military wars against Indian people all across a much earlier North America did tribes have to become so vocal and to so forcefully defend themselves as they did during the Termination Era. Termination meant the end of a tribe as a known and recognized group with sovereign rights that had been spelled out in treaty after treaty and agreement after agreement with the United States. Termination meant the breaking of every treaty ever made with indigenous, sovereign nations. However, in exchange for this dismantling, tribes would receive thousands of dollars. The United States government would treat Indians as it did any other citizens in the country.

Although a number of tribes accepted the offer to terminate, they would later come to regret their decisions. Like other tribes, the Nez Perce Tribe had individual members who favored termination for its monetary benefits, but the majority opposed it because of our traditional concern for future Nez Perce generations.

In 1953, Dillon Myer, Commissioner of Indian Affairs, and his promoted the Howard Wheeler Act and encouraged the sale of Indian lands. He supported Public Law 280, a law that called for immediate termination of Indian responsibilities, which was, of course, just another even more blatant attempt to take land from the tribes. In spite of the rejection of termination, the government nevertheless passed a bill that permitted the sale of Indian land plots created by the Dawes Act.

Once again, white profiteers made enormous financial gains from lands that were supposed to be held in sacred trust exclusively for tribal members. Coupled with taxation upon tribal lands, many allotments were sold at this time. This policy not only proved devastating to Indian people throughout the United States, it profited only a very few non-Indians. Consequently, this policy was called the second Affirmative Action Plan, the Homestead Act being the first to benefit thousands of "white only" Americans that came West. Federal and state policies that endorse land reduction or exploitation of natural resources on reservations continue to rise up in various forms. The Nez Perce Tribe has consistently opposed the philosophy behind this kind of thinking, and we will continue to do so.

The Nez Perce Tribe found support from and participated in organizations such as the National Congress of American Indians (NCAI). Our alliances with other tribes helped strengthen our resolve to confront critical issues such as the sale of Indian lands. Allotment sales were strongly opposed by the NCAI. As time passed, however, many tribal allotments became so fractionalized that the lands were of little use to their owners. There were checks issued as small as ten cents for the sale of such allotments. When this occurred, the land would be sold to outside buyers who were, not coincidentally, non-Indians.

Another issue that faced the Nez Perce and other tribes from the 1950s well into 1970s was the Relocation Act. This Act not only deterred tribes from meeting their economic goals, it, too, was born in Congress with the idea of getting Indians off their reservations. If Indian people refused to sell their land, then perhaps they could be lured away. The relocation policy allowed individual tribal members to move anywhere in the United States and receive a living stipend good for about six months. Unfortunately, very few Indian people from reservations who agreed to relocate actually succeeded in finding decent jobs or adjusting to city life. Most people came home broke and demoralized—or ended up forced to live below the poverty line when their stipend ran out. Some few who had the resources and family support to overcome social obstacles were able to acquire new job skills.

Somewhat like the land grab of the allotment period, once again the U.S. governments, State and Federal, saw an opportunity to gain tribal lands and resources for private ownership and private industry. Many tribes have millions of acres in land and literally billions of dollars in resources waiting to be developed, but not for tribal benefit.

Allen Pinkham

Nez Perce tribal elder Roy White had this to say about the Termination Era.

In 1948 the [Nez Perce] constitution and bylaws were written up by Archie Phinney. Some of our scholars thought that what Archie had written up was something like how the Russians have theirs. The main thing was we were trying to get the people to understand that we needed to have a constitution and bylaws. Some of us were rabble rousers, and as we would go through the document we pointed out some of the things that were in there that we didn't like. These people formed the first Amendments Committee. They were Tony Whitman, George Miles, William Eneas, and myself. We got Dennis Williams to tell us what the old people used to have so we could fix up the amendments according to that.

A lot of people thought I was for termination, but I never supported termination. Those tribal members who supported termination, like my cousin, were students living off the reservation. The tribe did not support termination, and for about three to four years there was quite a squabble between the outside Indians and the tribal Indians. At that time some thought I was a spy for the other side. I would go see Caleb Whitman to see what he would think. He said, "If these people are honest about what they want on the reservation, then the only thing they can do is wake the Nez Perce people up to what they want. That is the only way this is going to happen."

The only way to wake up the people was by pushing that [termination]. Pushing termination had the effect of getting people together to keep our reservation.

We used to laugh about that later on: the only way to keep the reservation was to get our families, relatives, and friends mad at us. It was really something. One of the biggest General Councils we ever had was to find out if we wanted to be terminated or not. I believe every voting person on the reservation was there for that meeting. I think that is when we got our tags [badges] started so we could see who lived off the reservation and who lived on the reservation. Gosh, that meeting took forever and ever. People would get up and talk. The Chairman let the old people talk and express what their fears were. Their fears were that if we were terminated we wouldn't have any place to live anymore. They were afraid that our homes and lands would be taken from us. Those old people really had a lot in their heads. Most of them would speak in Nez Perce because they couldn't speak English. My old friends would ask me in Indian, "Why are you with them over there?" I told them, "Well, I'm a mugwamp, a tribal mugwamp." Some of my minister friends were mad at me. I think if everything had went the way it was going we probably would have been terminated.

THE SELF-DETERMINATION ERA AND THE

EDUCATION ACT OF 1975

President John F. Kennedy laid the ground work for the Education Act when he was able to educate Congress about Indian people and their unique status. The common phrase we use today, "goverment-to-government," began with Kennedy who was also a proponent of the Civil Rights Movement that led to the Civil Rights Act.

Later, in 1968, President Johnson declared, "We must affirm the rights of the first Americans to remain Indians while exercising their rights as Americans. We must affirm their rights to freedom of choice and self-determination." These words signaled yet another shift in federal Indian policy and initiated changes that are still in effect. Perhaps the "Self-Determination" policy is best illustrated by Public Law 93-638. The Indian Self-Determination and Education Act permits tribes to contract certain services (such as the management and development of their natural resources) from the federal government (primarily from the Bureau of Indian Affairs). Until the Kennedy-Johnson years, the BIA had managed *all* tribal programs and all business that was determined to be cumbersome and costly. The BIA held the paternalistic view that the tribes were incapable of handling their own affairs, that we needed the BIA to "think for" and "take care" of us. Self-Determination sought to end that paternalistic and patronizing way of thinking and to create a new, more realistic, and more efficient policy.

Giving more impetus than one could imagine to the Indian Self-Determination movement was President Nixon, who signed thirty-seven pieces of legislation, seventeen of which became law. Although most Americans associate Nixon's name and his presidency with his achievements in building bridges with China and for the disgrace associated with his impeachment, too few know of his efforts on behalf of Native Americans. In essence, Nixon's policies relinquished control of services formerly performed by the Bureau of Indian Affairs, such as law enforcement, education, and economic development, [and turned that control] over to the tribal governments.

What sets Nixon's Indian policy apart from those of previous administrations is that he endorsed a coherent and comprehensive plan in place of piecemeal reforms. Nixon properly identified and recognized Indians as a unique group. In 1974, the National Congress of American Indians declared, "The President's Indian Message of 1970 will likely go down in history as the singular outstanding Presidential proclamation in recognition of the unique relationship between Indian tribes and the Federal Government."

Nez Perce Executive Committee Chairman Sam Penney giving a salmon speech at Lewiston in 1999. (Photo courtesy of Antonio Smith.)

Unbeknown to many of the "radical" groups of the 1960s, including the American Indian Movement (AIM), Nixon had already begun a series of policies that would re-establish Indian sovereignty. When the island of Alcatraz was retaken from the Native American occupation in 1969, it was on Nixon's order that no one was to be fired on or violently treated.

Nixon's Indian policies pointed the way. They led directly to the development of tribal control of tribal resources by tribal governments while simultaneously holding the federal government accountable for its trust responsibilities under the treaties signed a century or more earlier. The Indian Tribal Government Tax Status Act of 1982 extends many of the same tax advantages to Indian tribes that the states enjoy, including the ability to issue tax-exempt bonds to finance governmental operations. Although many state and local groups adamantly oppose the continued recognition of tribal governments, the U.S. courts have reaffirmed Congress' intent to recognize the unique relationship between the federal government and Indian tribes.

While federal Indian policy continues to evolve, tribal governments continue to advocate for stronger government-to-government consultation as the best means of resolving disputes and of providing services for their people. Since 1968, each consecutive U.S. President has declared or adopted a commitment by Executive Order to honor this relationship as defined by treaty, congressional act, or U.S. court decision.

NEZ PERCE SELF DETERMINATION

The Nez Perce Tribe saw this national movement of self determination a little differently than others. Aside from the reality now facing the Nez Perce that it would be necessary to struggle, suffer, and fight to keep our treaty rights, the Nez Perce also knew that the trust doctrine/trust responsibility held by the U.S. government must always be maintained. "Self Determination" was voted down by the Nez Perce Tribal Executive Committee (NPTEC) several times, although it meant losing the chance to receive certain monies. Nevertheless, a positive effect rippled through Indian Country as a result of the Indian

Self-Determination and Education Act, simply because of the change in attitude towards all tribes as true sovereigns. As of 2002, the following Nez Perce programs and departments no longer filter through the BIA or Indian Health Service:

- ▲ Nimiipu Health
- ▲ Forestry
- ▲ Fisheries
- ▲ Education
- ▲ Land Operations

Additionally, and on its own initiative, the Tribe has moved to create other developments such as Forest Products, Enterprises, Clearwater River Casino, Coyote Casino, the Wolf Re-introduction Program, and the Nez Perce Horse Registry.

Former Nez Perce Tribal Executive Committee Chairman Allen Pinkham remarked that

> This time was a turning point for tribes that are self-determined or that want to be self determined. Tribes were planning and implementing their own social programs and economic development ventures. Many were successful; others were destined to fail. But it was an expression of tribal sovereignty. For the Nez Perce people it meant bringing many legal actions to the forefront and winning the majority of court cases concerning treaty rights. One of the most important court cases that the Tribe won was the fishing rights issue at Rapid River. Self-Determination policies also supported the tribe

in purchasing land in former tribal areas. Many tribes now take the initiative to develop their own natural resources.

Many tribal members have long worried that the policy of Self-Determination has the potential to become yet another form of termination by allowing the federal government to overlook the original treaties that are already in effect. As the Nez Perce Tribe continues to develop and create its own policies in concert with western economies and western industries, we must exercise great caution and care to protect and perpetuate the rights reserved to us in the Treaties of 1855, 1863, and in the 1893 Agreement.

I received my diploma from Lapwai High School. I received my college degree from Lewis-Clark State College. But I received my education from Spalding University (Sweathouse).

Solo Greene

Nez Perce sweat house in early 1900s. (Photo courtesy of Nez Perce National Historical Park.)

CHAPTER 7

HUNTING, FISHING, PASTURING

AND GATHERING

We didn't make the skies bring rain, we didn't make the roots and berries grow, we didn't make the salmon run. When it was time for the salmon to run, we moved down to the rivers, and when it was time for the foods and medicines to grow, we turned to the mountains. We moved in reference to the landscape and to the resources that nature provided to us.

Jaime Pinkham

Our people traveled with the seasons: in Washington we picked berries at Mt. Adams, in Oregon we camped at Wallowa Lake, in Montana we hunted buffalo. By the time my kids are adults, will they still have the privilege to exercise their treaty rights?

Kamelle Bourgeau

It is impossible to explain in this short space the true significance and real depth of our views regarding our hunting, fishing, and gathering rights. As we have previously observed, the importance of our ability to hunt, to fish, to gather, to camp and to utilize both our resources and our resource sites has always been and remains of paramount interest and of primary concern to our leaders, both past and present. Too few people realize that the Nez Perce War of 1877 was about preserving our rights to inhabit our homelands and protecting the burial sites and sacred places of our ancestors. Preservation matters are as much a part of our practice of hunting, fishing, and gathering as the ability to travel and to gain access to these areas.

Under its current leadership, the Nez Perce Tribe has established tribally operated programs for fish restoration both on the reservation and at our usual and accustomed sites; a wildlife program for the management and protection of wildlife; and a cultural resources program to protect and preserve historical and sacred sites as well as to preserve our language and oral history. In 1998, the Nez Perce Tribe established a Fish and Wildlife Commission constituted of elected tribal members. The Fish and Wildlife Commission is primarily responsible for advising and assisting tribal officials with important policy issues that affect our resources.

The Nez Perce Tribe is also a party to the Snake River Basin Adjudication lawsuit currently before the Idaho State District Court. This important lawsuit will decide the fate of our tribally reserved water rights. As the original inhabitants of this land, our use of this important resource predates all claims of other users. What the court decides will be of vital importance to the Nez Perce people.

As it expanded westward, the United States discovered native people already occupying the lands it desired. In the Northwest Ordinance of 1787, Congress promised that the "utmost good faith shall always be observed towards the Indians; their land and property shall never be taken from them without their consent; and in their property, rights and liberty, they shall never be invaded or disturbed, unless in just and

Nez Perce Tribal member, Jackie Carson, with a Rapid River Salmon. (Photo courtesy of Dan Landeen.)

Elizabeth Wilson and Agnes Moses gathering roots in 1965 near Weippe, Idaho. (Photo courtesy of Nez Perce National Historical Park.)

We used to always go and camp there [at Hanford]. We also camped up and down the river. Then all the sudden, we were forbidden to camp at Celilo. Those that had camps got paid money, so they could buy other homes to live in. That doesn't make it right. That was our fishing place. George Walker testified at Jesse Green's hearing about fishing. He wrote a long essay about fishing. The Nez Perce went to Celilo even before they had horses. They traveled on foot, but they always went there. They always made it there at that time of year to go and fish. Just like they would go hunt buffalo in Montana, on the Lo Lo Trail. They went to go get buffalo, buffalo hides, along with the meat. They had peace with the different tribes that were by the buffalo. They had a place to go for salmon, for roots, and a place to go for camas. Everything we had, we worked hard for. Our people led a hard life, gathering the different foods in the summer.

Beatrice Miles

lawful wars authorized by Congress; but laws founded in justice and humanity shall from time to time be made for preventing wrongs being done to them, and for preserving peace and friendship with them" (1 Stat. 50).

The United States recognized *Niimiipuu* sovereignty when it sought to enter into a treaty with our people in 1855. During the treaty negotiations, *Niimiipuu* leaders recognized the importance of their natural resources to their cultural survival—and to the survival of future generations of *Niimiipuu*. Consequently, the Nez Perce Tribe expressly reserved the exclusive right to take fish within its reservation as well as the right to take fish at all usual and accustomed places in common with the citizens of the United States. The treaty also acknowledges the right of the Nez Perce to hunt, to gather roots and berries, and to pasture horses and cattle upon open and unclaimed lands. For Nez Perce people, all natural resources are important cultural and spiritual resources. The two have always been intertwined.

During the Treaty Council at Walla Walla, Territorial Governor and Superintendant of Indian Affairs Issac I. Stevens repeatedly assured the *Niimiipuu* that they would be secure in these rights. After describing the fisheries and gathering rights on the Reservation, Stevens stated

> You will be allowed to pasture your animals on land not claimed or occupied by settlers, white men. . . . You will be allowed to go to the usual fishing places and fish in

common with the whites, and to get roots and berries and to kill game on land not occupied by the whites; all this outside the Reservation.

According to the record of the official proceedings of the Council in the Walla Walla Valley, Governor Stevens, addressing the reluctant Chief Looking Glass, said

> Looking Glass knows that in this reservation settlers cannot go, that he can graze his cattle outside of the reservation on lands not claimed by settlers, that he can catch fish at any of the fishing stations, that he can kill game and go to buffalo when he pleases, that he can get roots and berries on any of the lands not occupied by settlers.

In 1911, during the first session of the 62nd Congress of the United States, *Niimiipuu* accounts of the Treaty Council record that

> [t]he thing of the greatest interest to us at the time was the right and possession of the game and fish, and the fact that these were reserved to our people was considered as the greatest compensation for the cessions.

The Nez Perce Tribe's Treaty-Reserved Rights

The *Niimiipuu's* fishing, hunting, gathering, and pasturing rights (and all the associated rights they necessarily encompass) existed prior to the 1855 Treaty. As the United States Supreme Court was to eloquently state, these treaty rights were "a part of larger rights possessed by the Indians, upon the exercise of which there was not a shadow of impediment, and which were not much less necessary to the existence of the Indians than the atmosphere they breathed" (*United States v. Winans*, 1905). In addition, the Treaty of 1855 contains other reserved rights. For example, Article III also recognizes that the Tribe reserved the right to the Clearwater River and its tributaries within the Reservation, while at the same time ensuring that citizens of the United States would be able to access these rivers "for rafting purposes." Beyond rights expressly reserved by treaty, established case law recognizes that the Tribe reserved whatever tribal rights existed at the time that were not conveyed away.

I called my uncle Harrison, in 1963, and told him that I'm in jail at The Dalles. "I'm in jail because I am fishing down here on the river," and he said, "They can't arrest you, you have treaty rights down there at the river." So they sent Ted Little, who was the attorney for the Tribe at that time, and it started a court case for the Tribe on the Columbia. We won that case.

Loretta Halfmoon

I used to fish for a living on the Columbia River. In 1967 I was picked up seventeen times for fishing. We went to court for three days. At the trial we were able to prove that the Nez Perce had a right to fish that area.

Ip Sus Noot V (Jesse Green)

The Nez Perce Tribe's Treaty Rights Remain Unaffected by the 1863 Treaty and 1893 Agreement

The rights that the *Niimiipuu* reserved in the 1855 Treaty have been unaffected by subsequent agreements between the United States and the Tribe. The Treaty of 1863 states that "all the provisions of said treaty which are not abrogated or specifically changed by any article herein contained, shall remain the same to all intents and purposes as formerly, the same obligations resting upon the United States, the same privileges continued to the Indian outside of the reservation...." Later, in the 1893 Agreement between the Nez Perce and the United States, the government goes on to say that the "existing provisions of all former treaties with said Nez Perce Indian not inconsistent with the provisions of this agreement are hereby continued in full force and effect."

The *Niimiipuu* reserved other rights in the 1863 Treaty. Article 8, for example reserved Nez Perce rights to springs and fountains.

> The United States also agree to reserve all springs or fountains not adjacent to, or directly connected with, the streams or rivers within the lands hereby relinquished, and to keep back from settlement or entry so much of the surrounding land as may be necessary to prevent the said springs or fountains being enclosed; and, further, to preserve a perpetual right of way to and from the same, as water places, for the use in common of both whites and Indians.

Interpretation of the Treaty Reserved Rights

When interpreting Indian treaties, the courts have recognized that the treaties were written in English, and that the basis for the negotiations were not between parties of equal sophistication. Thus, the courts have developed rules, known as the canons of construction, for interpreting Indian treaties:

1. Indian treaties must be interpreted so as to promote their central purposes.

2. Treaties are to be interpreted as the Indians themselves would have understood them.
3. Indian treaties are to be liberally construed in favor of the Indians.
4. Ambiguous expressions are to be resolved in favor of the Indians.

ACCESS TO USUAL AND ACCUSTOMED

FISHING PLACES

Even before Washington became a state, treaty rights similar to those of the Nez Perce were being challenged. Frank Taylor, a homesteader who had acquired land on the Columbia River near Tumwater, built a fence along the site. The fence blocked access for Yakama Indians who had always fished there and had reserved their right to fish at all usual and accustomed places. The Supreme Court of the Washington Territory ordered Taylor to remove the obstruction because the treaty expressly protected the Yakamas' right to take fish (*United States v. Taylor*, 1877).

As the canning industry began to develop on the Columbia River, Indians were forced out of many of their traditional fishing sites. In 1894 the Yakama Indian agent complained to his superiors in Washington that "the disputed fishing rights of the Indians along the Columbia" had given him "a vast amount of trouble." At that time Indians were legal wards of the Department of Interior, and the federal government was obligated to defend them against white incursions on their rights, regardless of how the defenders really felt. In 1905 the courts in Washington State ruled in favor of the Winans Brothers Cannery in banning Indians from fishing sites on riverbank land it had purchased. The federal government appealed the case to the Supreme Court, which ruled in *United States v. Winans* that not only were the Indians guaranteed access to their ancient fishing grounds under the 1855 Treaty, but also that the treaty itself must always be interpreted as the Indians had originally understood it. The court held that "The right to resort to the fishing places in controversy was a part of larger rights possessed by the Indians, upon the exercise of which there was not a shadow of impediment, and which were not much less necessary to the existence of the Indians than the atmosphere they breathed."

One time we were watching some non-Indians fish the Selway River. I didn't have my gaff with me that day, I was just watching. After a while they gave me a hook and encouraged me to make a gaff pole and snag a salmon. I attached the hook to a four-foot willow and proceeded to catch a salmon. As soon as I caught one the people who had given me the hook went and got the game warden. They wanted me to be arrested. The game warden came, but all he did was measure the fish. He said I had the right to catch the fish because the Selway area was a "usual and accustomed place." This made all the non-Indians mad because they wanted me to be arrested.

Ron Oatman

We need the salmon for our future and for our children. We need the salmon because it is part of our lives and part of our history. The salmon is a part of us, and we are a part of it. Our children need to be able to feel what it is like to catch and eat salmon. They need to be able to experience that sense of respect that many of us have felt in past years. We used to fish for salmon at Asotin Creek, and I can remember as a young girl trying to catch a large salmon that I could see in the shallow water. I chased that large fish upstream for a long ways without being able to catch it. But I remember the feeling of awe I felt for those fish even at that age. I knew how beautiful the fish were and are.

Julia Davis

Another landmark case frequently cited is found in *United States v. Seufert* (1916), which involved Indian fishing rights at a particular location along the Columbia River. The Seuferts owned and operated canneries at Celilo. In the book *Wheels of Fortune*, Seufert tells the following story.

In the early 1900s Seufert caught two whites selling liquor illegally on his cannery property. He told the whites that if they were caught a second time, he would turn them over to the federal authorities. To get even with him, the bootleggers found an old fish wheel scow and gave it to Sam Williams, an Indian who lived near Celilo. The bootleggers towed the fish wheel to the end of Threemile Reef for Williams to operate. Seufert previously had a fish wheel at that site for several years. Upon finding this old broken down fish wheel, Seufert took a crew and had it removed. Sam Williams took Seufert to court and charged him with interfering with an Indian's fishing rights under the 1855 Treaty.

Seufert admitted that he was familiar with this treaty. He said that he knew the treaty had guaranteed Indians the right to fish in their usual and accustomed places along the Columbia River. He argued, however, that although the treaty guaranteed the Indians the right to fish in their usual and accustomed places, at the time the treaty was signed the Indians were using spears and dip nets, not fish wheels. He would let an Indian cross Seufert land to the Columbia River to fish with a spear and a dip net but not with a fish wheel scow. The court ruled that under the treaty Sam Williams had the right to use a fish wheel scow at the end of Three Mile Reef. The judge specifically said, "I see no reason why Indians may not be permitted to advance in the arts and sciences as well as any other people, and, if they can catch their supply of food fish by a more scientific and expeditious method, there exists no good reason they may not be permitted to do so. Even more, they ought to be encouraged to adopt the more modern and advanced ways of prosecuting their enterprises."

The United States Supreme Court (*Tulee v. State of Washington*, 1942) also held that where a tribe's treaty reserves the rights to take fish at all usual and accustomed fishing places, a state may not require tribal members to obtain state fishing licenses.

The United States Supreme Court has affirmed the "usual and accustomed" treaty fishing clause in no fewer than six written opinions.

In *Sohappy v. Smith*, U.S. District court Judge Robert Belloni ruled in 1969 that the states could not restrict Indian fishing except for clearly defined conservation purposes. This ruling was not new, but Belloni also declared that the states must regulate the fishery in such a way as to guarantee the Indians a "fair and equitable share" of the fish already guaranteed to them by the treaties. The first part of the decision disappointed state officials, but the second part provoked considerable apprehension. What did "fair and equitable" really mean? This question was answered in 1974 by Judge George Boldt in *U.S. v. Washington*, (1974) which was brought to the courts by Puget Sound fishing activists and has since been referred to as the "Boldt Decision."

The Boldt Decision decreed that half the catch destined for usual and accustomed fishing places must be reserved for the Indians. Judge Belloni ruled a year later that the same rule must apply on the Columbia River. Former Attorney General for the State of Washington, Slade Gorton, tried for years to undermine and overturn the Boldt Decision, but in 1979 the Supreme Court upheld Judge Boldt's original decision. More recently, former Senator Slade Gorton tried, on several occasions, to limit or quash the tribes' sovereign immunity status with the federal government.

The federal district courts have retained continuing jurisdiction to protect the treaty rights that are the subject matter of these cases. In *U.S. v. Oregon*, the parties negotiated the Columbia River Fish Management Plan. The plan acts as a framework "within which the parties may exercise their sovereign powers in a coordinated and systematic manner in order to protect, rebuild, and enhance upper Columbia River fish runs while providing harvests for both treaty Indian and non-Indian fisheries." The parties are currently attempting to negotiate a successor to that management plan.

In interpreting these 1855 treaties, federal courts have established a large body of case law that sets forth certain fundamental principles (also known as "the conservation standards"). These principles include those that follow below. For state and federal government regulation of fishing rights to be permissible it must be demonstrated

1. that the regulation is reasonable and necessary for conservation of the resource
2. that the regulation in its application to Indians is necessary in the interests of conservation

One of our concerns as a tribe is that we put millions of fish back into the rivers and many people benefit from our efforts, yet when the salmon arrive back in our rivers we are limited on the amount of fish we can harvest.

James Holt

Even when I was a boy we got into the habit of hiding our fishing gear because of the fear of being hassled by the local law enforcement officials. It was always a touch and go situation. I can remember walking up the railroad tracks near Lapwai Creek. My father would have his pole between the rails on the ground, and he would have the hook tied to it in his hip pocket, and that's the way we packed our poles back and forth to the creek. We would do the same thing when we went over to Asotin up Ten Mile Creek. We always had to hide our fishing activities from the local law enforcement because they didn't want us fishing. Many times we used to fish at night even when we were gaffing for suckers so we could avoid being harassed.

Wilfred Scott

When our old people didn't have supermarkets or canneries, they relied on the salmon harvest for their survival. That reliance was part of their spiritual being. That is why the Indian people always give thanks to the air, water, and animals—because they relied on these things to survive.

Wilfred Scott

Elmer Crow at Rapid River. (Photo courtesy of Jeremy Five Crows.)

3. that the regulation is not discriminate against Indians exercising treaty rights, either on its face or as applied
4. that all measures have been taken to restrict non-Indian activities before treaty rights may be regulated and that
5. voluntary tribal conservation measures are inadequate for achieving the conservation purpose.

THE NEZ PERCE AND RAPID RIVER

Regardless of what treaties have been signed or what state and federal court cases have ruled, Native Americans are still confronted with conflicts over fishing rights. The Nez Perce are no exception. One of our "usual and accustomed" fishing places is Rapid River, a tributary of the Salmon River near Riggins, Idaho. Historically, several Nez Perce bands (particularly the White Bird and Looking Glass bands) fished this river for salmon. Fish were primarily caught with gaffs until the 1970s when dip nets became popular. The account provided below briefly summarizes the conflict that occurred between the State of Idaho and the Nez Perce Tribe regarding the Rapid River salmon fishery. Many Nez Perce believe that history repeats itself about every hundred years. The Rapid River controversy occurred a century after the Nez Perce fought the United States in the famous war of 1877.

Elmer Paul at Rapid River. (Photo courtesy of Diane Mallickan.)

The results from the court cases that issued from the Rapid River incidents that Judge Reinhardt ruled on in district court in Grangeville have become an important part of the Nez Perce Tribe's legal history. The case never went further than district court and many people are not aware of the decision that was made. Judge Reinhardt, in dismissing those cases, made two critical points. The first was that the state had made an attempt to prohibit Nez Perce treaty-fishing rights without consulting with the Tribe. The second major point was that the decision reaffirmed the Tribe's fishing rights at its "usual and accustomed places" off the reservation in accordance with the Treaty of 1855. The Rapid River episode is an important piece of legal history and resulted in an important piece of law that pertains directly to the Tribe.

Doug Nash

One time at Rapid River I spotted someone up on the hill looking down at us fishing. I went to the truck and got out my rifle with the scope and was surprised to see a Game and Fish officer looking back at me through his own rifle and scope.

Julius Ellenwood

During the late 1970s and early 1980s the Nez Perce Tribe came into conflict with the State of Idaho regarding the rights of the Nez Perce to harvest salmon from Rapid River. Without any consultation with the Nez Perce Tribe, the State of Idaho decided to institute a closure of the Rapid River salmon fishery. The State's position was that the salmon were in "eminent peril" and there were too few fish returning to propagate the species. It was also the State's contention that the Indians were one of the primary causes for the decline of the fishery.

The Nez Perce fishermen who traditionally fished Rapid River contended that

1. the fishery was still strong
2. that Indians were not the main cause for the decline of the salmon fishery, and that they should not be blamed for the demise of the salmon and
3. that the closure was a direct violation of the fishing rights stipulated in the Treaty of 1855.

When the State of Idaho attempted to impose the closure, opinions varied among tribal members about the best course of action. One of the prevalent opinions was that the Tribe should avoid a controversy over the state's fishing closure and go along with its recommendation. The Tribe's indecision about what to do subsequently led to the formation of a fishermen's committee composed of Nez Perce fishermen who traditionally fished at Rapid River every year. Their intent was to oppose the State's recommendations to close the salmon fishery.

The fishermen involved directly in the Rapid River controversy have probably never been given the credit they deserve. Those people had to face many obstacles including displays of arms and force. The fact that whole families were involved made an important statement to the State about how the Nez Perce people felt about their treaty rights.

Doug Nash

I was one of the little boys running around down at Rapid River when all that madness was going on. The big thing there was protection of the treaty rights, and that was basically preached to us as kids. You know, people like Waddo getting choked by the police and all these things of what was happening over fishing at the time at Rapid River. [It] was not so much knowing but watching these men and all these people fighting over fish and how important that was to them.

Anthony Johnson

As recently as the 1970s you could stop at the stores in Riggins and see signs that said, "No dogs, no cats, no Indians allowed." They were especially prevalent between 1979 and 1980 when we were having trouble with the State of Idaho at Rapid River.

A.K. Scott

Several meetings were held, a spokesman was chosen, and strategies were formulated.

During this time, however, actions against Nez Perce fishermen at Rapid River by local vigilante groups escalated. On numerous occasions fishermen were harassed, run off the road, shot at, and threatened with violence. The first action of The Fishermen's Committee was to go to Rapid River and exercise Nez Perce tribal fishing rights. This first group of twenty-eight people who decided to fish at Rapid River included women and children. When they arrived, they were confronted and outnumbered by the presence of State of Idaho law enforcement officials. The fishermen wanted to avoid any confrontation that could lead to violence or loss of life, so in a solemn moment they decided to join hands and say a prayer for guidance. The leader of the committee let the others know that "power did not come from guns or numbers, but that power came from the convictions of the people." The group leader also said that the Nez Perce ancestors and elders were with them and that if they were strong things would work out. One week later, over 300 Nez Perce showed up to support the fishermen in their effort to protect their treaty rights at Rapid River.

With so many people on both sides active and involved and tempers running strong, the chances for an escalation into violence were very real. Nez Perce Tribal Executive Committee members and a representative from The Fishermen's Committee were asked by a federal arbitrator to meet with the Governor of Idaho in Boise to help resolve the issue. At that meeting, the state proposed that the Nez Perce be allowed to exercise their treaty fishing rights in what the state representatives called a "simulated fishery." The Nez Perce representatives said that this proposal sounded all right, but could the state please explain what it meant by "simulated fishery."

The State explained that the Indians would be allowed to dipnet and gaff on the river, but the poles would not have nets on them, and the gaffs would be devoid of hooks. That way, the State explained, the Indians could still exercise their treaty rights without harvesting any fish, and both sides would be satisfied. The State representatives said that the State would allow the Chairman of the Nez Perce Tribal Executive Committee to catch one fish. The catch would be accompanied with a media photo session so that the Tribe could get credit for resolving the issue in a peaceable manner.

It is difficult to imagine that such an insulting proposal would be seriously put forward today by the State of Idaho, and almost impossible to imagine that the Nez Perce Tribe would entertain it. The Rapid River proposal exemplified the State's ignorance and its lack of understanding of the 1855 Treaty and what actually constituted the legal rights of the Nez Perce people to fish at their "usual and accustomed places." Few state leaders understood that these rights extend to locations outside our reservation boundaries.

Needless to say, the State's proposal was soundly rejected, and the representative of The Fishermen's Committee let the governor know that the Committee was insulted by the proposal. He said that he was going back to Rapid River to fish and that if he ended up dying because of his convictions, then so be it. Later that day the State withdrew the proposal and compromised with the Tribe by proposing that tribal members fish at selected times.

This compromise temporarily diffused the situation and was partly satisfactory to both sides. The compromise ultimately failed, however, because the next year the State's new management team decided again to impose a fishing closure at Rapid River. The Fishermen's Committee, which had never totally disbanded, rallied again and voiced strong opinions for opposing the State's proposal. The Nez Perce Tribal Executive Committee passed a resolution to support The Fishermen's Committee and to continue with the practice of exercising our treaty rights at Rapid River.

This action resulted in strong shows of force by the State of Idaho at Rapid River and over eighty tribal fishermen ended up being arrested for various violations. The most common charges filed against fishermen were illegal fishing, illegal possession of fish, and failure to show up in court. In fact, one Nez Perce boy of seven was arrested after he had caught his first salmon. It was common to see fully camouflaged SWAT teams driving up and down the roads. Many of the teams set up observation stations above the river. By this time several national newspapers and outside environmental justice groups were following the story. High profile lawyers from across the country volunteered their legal services to represent tribal members in court. Several tribal members were jailed in Grangeville for various lengths of time during those years.

In all, thirty-three pending court cases against Nez Perce fishermen were lumped into one court case that was decided by Judge Reinhardt in

The salmon is an integral part of our tribal and family traditions. Even white people can understand the importance of preserving family and cultural traditions. How can I explain to people what it means to me to go down to Rapid River and dip net for salmon? How can I describe the feeling of putting that dip net in the water and feeling the power of that salmon. . . ? It is something that you feel in your heart, and it is something that you hope can be taught to our children and future generations. As Nez Perce people, we need to fight to save the salmon.

Aaron Miles

The first salmon ceremony and other ceremonies are important because they teach us about the value of life and the value of animals and our relationship to them. The ceremonies remind us that we have a responsibility to the animals, just as they have a responsibility to us. The first salmon feast was a very serious occasion, especially for the fishing families and the fishermen themselves. They had to make sure they had the right songs and that the ceremony was done correctly as far as which foods were introduced in what order. The food was prepared in the traditional way and also served in the traditional way, which was on the floor on the tule mats. Only certain people were allowed to serve, and special songs were sung as the food was brought out. It was then announced in native language that "Now you will taste the salmon," "Now you will taste the meat," "Now you will taste the berry." It was a very important ritual that recognized the importance of each one of those food groups within the Nez Perce life.

Carla HighEagle

District Court at Grangeville, Idaho, in 1982. Judge Reinhardt threw out all thirty three cases and ruled that the State of Idaho had not consulted with the tribes about imposing restrictions on the Rapid River fishery and that in the future the Tribe and the State would have to work together to determine how that fishery should be managed. Judge Reinhardt's decision, based on the language in the 1855 Treaty, reaffirmed the Tribe's right to fish at its "usual and accustomed places."

Since that time the State of Idaho and the Tribe have worked together to manage this fishery and there have been years when the fishery has been closed. Hopefully, our joint salmon restoration efforts will be such that this fishery will someday fully recover so that Nez Perce people can continue to use Rapid River as a place to honor the salmon.

CAMPING RIGHTS

The Nez Perce Tribe's treaty-reserved rights include the right to camp while hunting, fishing, and gathering. Many of our traditional camping sites on federal lands have now been "developed," and the Tribe and the United States have entered into subsequent agreements to protect our Tribe's treaty-reserved rights.

Court decisions have also recognized that the Tribe's treaty-reserved rights include the ability to erect structures at our usual and accustomed fishing sites (*Sohappy v. Hodel*, 1990).

HUNTING

Article III of the Nez Perce Treaty of 1855 reserves the Tribe's fishing rights and goes on to reserve "the privilege of hunting, gathering roots and berries, and pasturing their horses and cattle upon open and un-claimed land." Governor Stevens explicitly assured Looking Glass that he could "graze his cattle outside of the reservation on lands not claimed by settlers," that he could "kill game and go to buffalo" whenever he pleased, and that he could "get roots and berries on any of the lands not occupied by settlers."

In a case involving a Nez Perce Tribal member hunting on National Forest lands outside the boundaries of the Reservation, but within the exterior boundaries of the lands the Tribe ceded to the United States, the Idaho Supreme Court held in *State of Idaho v. Arthur* (1953) that the rights reserved by the Nez Perce Indians in 1855, which have never passed from them, to hunt upon open and unclaimed land still exist unimpaired and that they are entitled to hunt at any time of the year in any of the lands ceded to the federal government though such lands are outside of their reservation.

While that case dealt with tribal treaty hunting within the ceded lands, courts have recognized (*State of Washington v. Buchanan*, 1999) that these rights may extend outside the Tribe's ceded territory as well where there is evidence that the Tribe's aboriginal hunting grounds extended outside the ceded territory.

For the Nez Perce Tribe, the record of Governor Stevens assuring Looking Glass that these rights would extend to buffalo country is clear evidence that both the Tribe and the United States understood the rights to hunt on open and unclaimed land would extend to areas even outside the ceded territory.

Although most of the Supreme Court cases regarding treaties have arisen from fishing issues, the Nez Perce Tribe in 1855 did enter into a hunting treaty with the Blackfeet Tribe in Montana. The 1855 Treaty with the Blackfeet contains the agreements between a number of tribes (including the Nez Perce Tribe) who occupied, "for the purposes of hunting, the territory on the Upper Missouri and Yellowstone Rivers." The treaty recites that peace shall perpetually exist between the U.S. and these tribes (Article 1) and between the tribes themselves (Article 2). The Treaty establishes that the Blackfeet Nation consents and agrees that an area within the Blackfoot Territory, as described in the Treaty of Fort Laramie,

> shall be a common hunting ground for ninety nine years, where all nations, tribes and bands of Indians, parties to this treaty, may enjoy equal and uninterrupted privileges of hunting, fishing and gathering fruit, grazing animals, curing meat and dressing robes. . . . Provided, That the western Indians [including Nez Perce], parties to this treaty, may hunt on the trail leading down the Muscle Shell to the Yellowstone. . . and that the rights of the western Indians to a whole or a part of the common hunting-ground, derived from occupancy and possession, shall not be affected by this article, except so far as said rights may be determined by the treaty of Laramie.

The United States Court of Claims, in analyzing and rejecting claims of several tribes for damages resulting from the failure of the United States to protect the bison and other game from destruction on the common hunting ground, held that

> Assuredly no article of the treaty may be cited wherein the Government obligated itself to maintain this enormous acreage of land as a game preserve for the Indians for 99 years. The right accorded was a permissive one and its continued existence was dependent upon numerous factors over which neither the Government nor the Indians could possibly have control. This treaty cannot be read in any way or by any terms guaranteeing to the Indians maintenance of the status quo for almost a century.

In *Blackfeet v. United States* (1935) the Court, relying on the plain language of the Treaty with the Blackfeet in light of the canons of construction of Indian law, concluded that the agreement remained in effect only 99 years, and even during that time period gave the tribes limited rights. Thus, *after* the expiration of this agreement, the Nez Perce Tribe's hunting rights are those defined in the Nez Perce Treaty of 1855.

The Nez Perce Tribe and its members continue to exercise our treaty reserved hunting and gathering rights on all federally owned and tribally-owned lands within the 1855 Treaty boundaries and at all usual and accustomed places within our aboriginal territories. Our tribal members have been cited numerous times into state courts for exercising these rights. The majority of cases, however, continue to be dismissed in recognition of our treaty-reserved rights. The harassment of tribal hunters and gatherers is an ongoing problem, a problem that tribal government and tribal legal counsel deal with on a regular basis.

Finally, to further insure our ability to exercise our rights, the Nez Perce Tribe is actively involved in the restoration of the natural environment. This involvement takes many forms at many levels in terms of management, enforcement, legal strategy, and clean up. Habitat restoration—the rebuilding of the fish runs, the protection of elk and wildlife habitat, as well protection for traditional plant foods and plant medicines—are the goals of these efforts. The Nez Perce Tribe realizes that the fish and the water, so important to our survival for thousands of generations, must be restored to health and perpetuated for the benefit of all people. To accomplish restoration, the Tribe has developed a multilevel approach at the government-to-government level and also initiated a grassroots approach to cleaning the environment.

All Treaty Rights Must be Viewed Together

In addressing specific disputes, courts have often focused on individual treaty rights. Yet, history, the treaty minutes, and the understanding of tribal members was that these rights were often exercised simultaneously—a journey would not be a fishing trip *or* a hunting expedition, but rather, any journey would likely include all of these activities and require camping along the way. Thus, the same rules or canons of construction apply to the Tribe's treaty-reserved pasturing and gathering rights. Tribal members actively exercise all of these rights, from gathering roots and berries, to gathering tipi poles and wood, to pasturing their animals.

Responsible Exercise of Treaty Rights

The *Niimiipuu* recognize that with rights come responsibilities. The Nez Perce pass down from generation to generation the honor, respect, and stewardship for their treaty-reserved resources. The Nez Perce Tribe exercises their sovereignty by enacting rules and regulations addressing their treaty rights. The Nez Perce Tribe's Conservation Enforcement officers are responsible for enforcing these rules.

With Idaho, as Larry Greene, Sr. was called, it was, "I'm going hunting. Are you going to sweat, because anybody who goes hunting with me has to sweat because if you don't the animals will smell you." Being a little guy, I can't even recall how old I was, but coming out and getting done sweating I would say, "I went eight rounds!" and he would say, "That's good. You can go hunting with me." Basically, taking yourself to the point of dehydration to prove the fact that you could go hunting with him.

Anthony Johnson

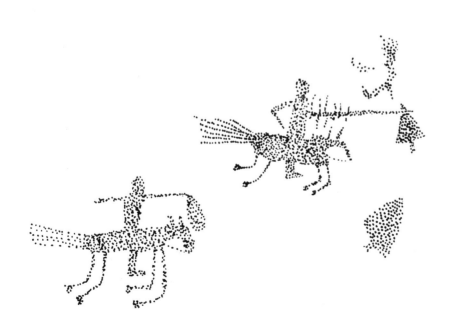

Chapter 8

The Nez Perce Tribe Today

The Nez Perce Tribe plays a crucial role in the management and the preservation of cultural and natural resources, the operation of health and judicial systems, and the development of economies within our reservation boundaries. The Tribe still retains certain rights to resources within its ceded lands, which include the Columbia River and its tributaries in the states of Oregon, Montana, Idaho, and Washington.

The challenge facing the Nez Perce Tribe, the U.S. government, states, counties, and cities is finding a way to effectively reconcile the many principles of law that impact our government-to-government relationships.

Land Base

The land and its resources have provided the basis for the Nez Perce way of life for countless generations. The lessons we learn from nature and the environment about its conservation and care are carried forward to each generation. The land defines who we are, and we recognize the unity of the physical and spiritual universe. We still move with the seasons, managing their bounty and diversity with an explicit respect for maintaining a balance with our surroundings. We celebrate Mother Earth's annual rebirths and offer thanks for the first foods she provides to us in recognition of our promise with the Creator and with the land. We possess a land ethic based on use, reciprocity, and balance.

When Lewis and Clark first came into contact with the Nez Perce, our people controlled vast territories. These lands were not individually owned but collectively used for the benefit of our families and bands. This method of collective land ownership could not be accommodated by the European legal system at the time, and, since it had no label, the term "Indian title" was developed to describe aboriginal tribal ownership of real property. The legal significance of Indian title was that Indian title could only be extinguished by the United States, and this, of course, was done using a number of different techniques.

Del White, Nez Perce tribal member at Big Hole Memorial. (Photo courtesy of Antonio Smith.)

I see so many good things going on for our young people. I am really happy and proud of this. We have a lot of good schools and education. Our young people are becoming what our elders have talked about: our children's children.

Horace Axtell

Typically, Indian treaties resulted in tribes surrendering vast areas of land to the United States. When that happened, the Indian title was extinguished. If a reservation, comprised of part of the land previously owned by the tribe, was set aside for tribal use, the land so reserved continued to be held by Indian title.

In later years, the term "trust land" evolved out of the relationship that had developed between the United States and Indian tribes. Through treaties and agreements Indian tribes became dependent upon the United States for protection and subject to plenary governmental power of Congress. Nevertheless, the United States, by those same treaties and agreements, obligated itself to provide tribes with education, medical care, and housing.

The Nez Perce Tribe holds beneficial title to trust land. This beneficial title allows the Tribe to use the land, to lease it, to build on it, and, essentially, do anything—except sell it. The Tribe cannot sell its trust land because it does not own the legal title. The United States owns that title, and it would require an act of Congress to sell tribal trust property. Consequently, trust land enjoys certain immunities from state or local taxation, zoning laws, and the like.

Grande Ronde River. (Photo courtesy of Dan Landeen.)

NEZ PERCE GOVERNMENT

In 1923 James Stuart, who had been an interpreter for Alice Fletcher during the allotment years, became the first president of the Nez Perce Home and Farm Association. This group formed the basis for a tribal council that was organized in 1927. In the 1930s federal Indian policy with regard to Indian affairs focused on providing assistance to Indian tribes in organizing representative forms of government. The Bureau of Indian Affairs provided assistance in drafting tribal constitutions and developing tribal governmental structures. The Nez Perce Tribe presently operates under a constitution and bylaws originally adopted in 1948 and which subsequently have been amended several times.

The Nez Perce Constitution delegates most governmental functions to the Nez Perce Tribal Executive Committee, which is comprised of nine tribal members from the reservation elected at large for three year terms. Three positions on the Executive Committee are elected each year by the General Council, all enrolled members of the Tribe over the age of 18. Executive Committee members can run for reelection and serve several terms. The General Council meets twice a year, in May and September, for the purpose of hearing reports from the Executive Committee. Internal Executive Committee elections, for the positions of Chairman, Vice-Chair, and other offices are held during the Committee's May meetings.

I think our tribes are doing the best they can. They have to fight everybody all the way. This is where I think they should understand the treaty and be strong that way.

Gladys Allen

2001 Nez Perce Tribal Executive Committee Back L-R: Wilfred "Scotty" Scott, Allen Slickpoo, Jr., Carla HighEagle, Justin Gould, and Jake Whiteplume. Front: Julia Davis, Anthony Johnson, Sam Penney, and Jennifer Oatman-Brisbois. (Photo courtesy of the Nez Perce Tribe.)

We need Nez Perce people speaking on behalf of Nez Perce people and they need to be knowledgeable about these treaty rights. I think this makes us a stronger community to defend the basis of our treaty rights and, really, to protect them into the future. . . .

Government is about citizenship, and it's about how people can really help to define and create a better future for their community.

Jaime Pinkham

To me, we could take that treaty right further in a way where we can become an authority in that area. Whether its fishing or for health and education. We need to expand our governmental and sovereign roles. We need to take a stronger stance for licensing of non-Indians hunting and fishing on the reservation. We need to have a greater role in forest management in our ceded lands. We need to have an expanded role in the education of our children in the schools here and to educate the non-Indians about our way of life. Also in the areas of health, we need to really look at the fundamental problems of our health system and really strengthen that.

James Holt

The Nez Perce Tribal Government, like many tribal governments, began on a very small scale. Today, the Nez Perce Tribe employs about 900 individuals and has an operating budget of approximately $18 million. (An organizational chart of the Nez Perce Tribe can be found at the back of the book. The chart describes our governmental departments as well as our tribal enterprises and tribally-owned businesses that provide additional revenue to the Tribe).The Nez Perce Tribe also has an aggressive land acquisition program through which tribal lands inside and outside the current reservation boundaries, lost through the treaty and allotment process, are being reacquired.

Today, over 3,300 individuals are enrolled as members of the Nez Perce Tribe. Elected tribal leaders represent the Tribe on wide variety of issues in interactions with federal, state, and local governments, as well as other tribal governments. In 2001, the Nez Perce Tribe passed an amendment to the voting requirements that now allow tribal members living anywhere to come home and vote in the bi-annual General Council meetings. The Tribe regulates the exercise of treaty-reserved rights to hunt and to fish by tribal members within and outside of the Nez Perce Reservation. The Tribe also exercises broad criminal jurisdiction over Indians within the reservation and civil jurisdiction over non-Indians whose actions affect the political integrity, economic well-being, or the health and welfare of the Tribe.

It is the obligation, as well as the commitment, of the Nez Perce Tribal Executive Committee to ensure a viable future for the Tribe and its members. This means providing a full measure of governmental services to the tribal community, protecting and preserving treaty rights and tribal sovereignty, and continuing to create and to keep secure a sound economic base.

NEZ PERCE TRIBE

GOVERNMENT-TO-GOVERNMENT CONSULTATION

The United States' trust obligation includes a substantive duty to consult with a tribe in decision-making to avoid adverse impacts on treaty resources and a duty to protect tribal treaty-reserved rights "and the resources on which those rights depend" (*Klamath Tribes v. U.S.*, 1996). The duty ensures that the United States conduct meaningful consultation "in advance with the decision maker or with intermediaries with clear authority to present tribal views to the. . . decision maker" (*Lower Brule Sioux Tribe v. Deer*, 1995).

Nez Perce Tribe Executive Committee in 1968 at Lapwai. Left to right, Lynus Walker, Angelo Idarola, Phil Types, Maurice Slickpoo, Moses Thomas, Richard Halfmoon, Robert Strong, Lee Seth, Shirley Rickman. (Photo courtesy of Nez Perce Tribe.)

Further, Executive Order 13175 provides that each "agency shall have an accountable process to ensure meaningful and timely input by tribal officials in the development of regulatory policies that have tribal implications." According to the President's April 29, 1994 Memorandum regarding Government-to-Government Relations with Native American Tribal Governments, federal agencies "shall assess the impacts of Federal Government plans, projects, programs, and activities on tribal trust resources and assure that Tribal government rights and concerns are considered during the development of such plans, projects, programs, and activities." As a result, federal agencies must proactively protect tribal interests, including those interests associated with tribal culture, tribal religion, tribal subsistence, and tribal commerce. Meaningful consultation with the Nez Perce Tribe is a vital component of this process.

Consultation is the formal process of negotiation, cooperation, and mutual decision-making between two sovereigns: the Nez Perce Tribe (NPT) and the United States (including all federal agencies). Consultation is the process that ultimately leads to the development of a decision—not just a process or a means to an end. The most important component of consultation is the ultimate decision.

Consultation does not mean notifying the Tribe that an action will occur, requesting written comments on that prospective action, and then proceeding with the action. In this scenario the decision is not affected. "Dear Interested Party" letters are not consultation.

An Executive Committee's oath is to swear to uphold the Constitution of the United States and to protect the treaty rights. To me, that means not negotiating them away but standing firm and saying now we will not give this up.

Anthony Johnson

I think we need to do a lot of redefining. . . not only of tribal council, but of the various departments and programs we have. We might need to seriously consider incorporating the seventh generation philosophy more than we do.

Arthur Taylor Jr.

The vision is that we maintain and build upon the successes we have enjoyed the past few years. When you look to the vision, you look to where you came from. You remember the sacrifices of the generations long before us.

Jaime Pinkham

It is equally important to understand that as a sovereign government, the Tribe may elect not to conduct government-to-government consultation or may decide to limit the scope of their consultation as needed.

The primary objectives of consultation are

1. to insure that the Nez Perce Tribal Executive Committee (NPTEC) understands the technical and legal issues necessary to make an informed policy decision
2. to insure federal compliance with treaty and trust obligations, as well as other applicable federal laws and policies impacting tribal culture, religion, subsistence, and commerce
3. to improve policy-level decision-making of both NPTEC and federal government
4. to facilitate bilateral decision-making between two sovereigns (co-management of resources)
5. to guarantee the protection of NPT resources, culture, religion, and economy
6. to insure compliance with tribal laws and policies
7. to develop and achieve mutual decisions through a complete understanding of technical and legal issues, and
8. to improve the integrity of federal/tribal decisions.

THE PROCESS OF CONSULTATION

Consultation works through both technical and policy-level meetings to distinguish between technical and policy issues. Consultation allows for proper technical-level staff consultation followed by policy-level

Nez Perce Tribe Executive Committee in the 1970s. Left to right, Angus Wilson, Harrison Lott, Mose Thomas, Phil Types, Richard Halfmoon, Ip Sus Noot V, Tim Wheeler, David Miles, Richard Ellenwood. (Photo courtesy of Nez Perce Tribe.)

consultation for those issues that remain unresolved (or for those issues that are clearly only capable of being resolved at the policy level). Consultation is the process of coming to common understanding of the technical and legal issues that affect (or are affected by) a decision, and then using this common understanding to formulate a decision.

Meaningful consultation requires that federal agencies and tribes understand their respective roles. Meaningful consultation requires that both sides have a basic understanding of the legal underpinnings of the government-to-government relationship, including the responsibility of the federal government under the Trust Doctrine. In addition, federal agencies will benefit from some understanding of tribal culture, tribal perspectives, tribal worldviews, and tribal treaty rights. Tribal governments must understand the policy decision-making authority of the federal agency. Tribal governments must understand the non-tribal politics of the federal agency decision that consultation will affect.

In these examples, it is critical to note that a tribal government cannot understand the politics of the federal agency decision without personal communications. Similarly, the federal agency cannot understand the Tribe's issues and concerns unless staff members of the federal agency meet with the Tribe to discuss those issues and concerns. Without communication, consultation is meaningless, and a mutual decision is difficult or impossible to reach.

The consultation process works like this:

1. Federal agency contacts NPTEC or its appointed point-of-contact to notify the Tribe of an impending project proposal or to conduct an activity that may or may not impact a tribal resource.
2. NPTEC responds that this issue is important and that it would like to initiate consultation. NPTEC requests that federal agency technical experts meet with tribal technical staff (or NPTEC requests a policy level meeting).
3. Consultation has been initiated. Technical staffs meet. Technical and legal issues are discussed; the result is that tribal staff members understand the proposal and federal agency staff members understand at the technical level why this proposed activity is of concern to the Tribe. Such a procedure allows respective technical staffs to brief respective policy entities and to provide informed opinions and recommendations.

As a young tribal member, I had very little knowledge of our tribal government system. I really did not know what services the tribal departments and programs provided. I also did not comprehend the vast amount of work being conducted by the Tribe in areas of natural resource management. Today, I feel that it is one of my duties, as a tribal natural resource employee, to assist our youth in understanding environmental issues, to help them build a sense of responsibility for the environment, and to inform them of the educational and career opportunities related to natural resources that may become beneficial to themselves and the Nez Perce Tribe.

Patrick Sobotta

4. Tribal staff briefs NPTEC. Consultation is initiated between policy level decision-makers from both the Tribe and the federal agency.
5. Additional meetings are held, if necessary, leading up to the decision.
6. The federal agency and the Tribe formulate a decision. Assurances are made that the decision is consistent with federal laws and tribal laws and policies. This means the decision is consistent with applicable natural and cultural resource laws and policies. For the Nez Perce Tribe specifically, it means the decision protects the resources to which the Nez Perce Tribe has specific treaty-reserved rights and enables continued practice of tribal religious, cultural, and subsistence activities.

These steps may be adapted to suit the needs of the decision-making process leading to the formulation of a decision.

Nez Perce Inter-Governmental Relationships Today

The federal trust responsibility imposes an affirmative duty on federal agencies to safeguard treaty-reserved natural resources, which are of critical importance to tribal self-government and prosperity. Whenever a federal agency proposes an action that will impact those resources, the agency is obligated to engage in meaningful government-to-government consultation with the Nez Perce Tribe. Ideally, the consultation will be on-going throughout the life of the project and result in mutual decision-making. The Nez Perce Tribe has adopted guidelines to aid in government-to-government consultations. These guidelines detail the process the Tribe would like to follow to insure effective communication, and to insure the full consideration of resource issues significant to the Tribe.

The Nez Perce Tribe has established working relationships with several government agencies including the National Park Service, the Bureau of Indian Affairs, Indian Health Service, the U.S. Department of the Interior, the U.S. Environmental Protection Agency, Washington State Department of Ecology, the Bonneville Power Agency, and the U.S. Department of Energy. A brief discussion of some of these working relationships that presently exist between the Tribe and these agencies follows below.

UNITED STATES FOREST SERVICE

As a result of the Treaty of 1855, the Nez Perce Tribe ceded huge tracts of our aboriginal territory to the United States in exchange for such reserved treaty rights as "the exclusive right of taking fish in all the streams…running through or bordering" our reservation. We "further secured…the right of taking fish at all usual and accustomed places in common with citizens of the Territory; and or erecting temporary buildings for curing, together with the privilege of hunting, gathering roots and berries, and pasturing" our "horses and cattle upon open and unclaimed land."

Tribal members continue to exercise these treaty-reserved rights in areas that are today administered by the United States Forest Service (USFS). In January 1992, the Nez Perce Tribe entered into a unique Memorandum of Understanding (MOU) with five national forests:

- ▲ the Umatilla National Forest
- ▲ the Clearwater National Forest
- ▲ the Nez Perce National Forest
- ▲ the Payette National Forest and
- ▲ the Wallowa-Whitman National Forest.

The 1992 Memorandum enabled the creation of a USFS-Nez Perce tribal liaison position to strengthen communications between the Tribe and the USFS.

Such a position has assisted the parties in "promoting" the furtherance of dialogue and coordination on contemporary natural resource issues not only of concern for the Nez Perce Tribe, but for all "American Indian Tribes."

The improved communication outlined in the MOU led to discussion between the parties about the need to allow tribal members to camp in National Forests while en route to a fishing, hunting, gathering, or grazing site—or while exercising a treaty right. These discussions led to another MOU signed (by tribal leaders, the Northern Region, Intermountain Region, and Pacific Region Foresters) in May of 1998. This MOU recognized the inherent right of tribal members to camp in areas where they have historically camped without paying USFS use fees and without length-of-stay obligations.

People always talk about "ecosystem management" and "holistic management." Too often I see those concepts focused on such things as sustainability of trees and forage (commercial enterprises). The sustainability of traditional foods and medicines are never discussed. For many of these people the sustainability of the salmon is not important. Many of these people are only interested in the sustainability of large commercial economies, such as grazing, mining and timber. So it's easy for other resources like the salmon to get pushed aside. For many the salmon and other natural resources are looked at as being in the way. Who is going to speak on behalf of the salmon? Up to this point, it has been the Indian people and some special interest groups who have been trying to get the voice of the salmon heard.

Jaime Pinkham

In addition to these agreements, the United States Forest Service and the Nez Perce Tribe participate in numerous collaborative land and resource management activities that benefit all public users, including fish and wildlife habitat improvement activities, cooperative law enforcement activities, cooperative fire management activities, cooperative watershed management activities, and forest and basin-wide planning. These efforts and others were made possible by visionary leaders who sincerely believed that mutually beneficial goals could be met by working closely and cooperatively together.

BONNEVILLE POWER AGENCY

The Nez Perce Tribe contracts with Bonneville Power Agency (BPA) to conduct various fisheries and wildlife projects related to impacts of the Columbia River power system. The Tribe's Department of Fisheries Resource Management has several projects underway funded by BPA. These projects include conservation enforcement and tributaries restoration. In particular, BPA has funded our habitat/watershed restoration activities in the Lochsa River, the South Fork of the Clearwater River, the Clearwater River tributaries, and (with the creation of the Nez Perce Tribal Hatchery) fall Chinook acclimation, the Northeast Oregon Hatchery, and many other research and monitoring projects of resident fish. These programs impact restoration for a variety of fish species, including Chinook salmon, coho salmon, rainbow trout, cutthroat trout, bull trout, and sturgeon.

The Conservation Resource Division works to provide optimum fish and wildlife conservation protection within the Nez Perce Reservation and Treaty of 1855 areas in order to enhance and sustain tribal fisheries, wildlife, and the natural ecosystem for the use of future generations.

The Habitat/Watershed Division focuses on protecting, restoring, and enhancing watersheds and all treaty resources. Our **Production Division** concentrates on using surplus adult fish and hatchery production to provide fish for natural spawning runs and to create harvest opportunities. Our **Research Division** provides information on population status, effectiveness of hatchery programs, smolt survival estimates, and fisheries management recommendations. Our **Resident Fish Division** attempts to conserve, restore, and recover native resident fish populations including sturgeon, Westslope Cutthroat trout, and bull trout.

The Nez Perce Tribe also has a **Precious Lands** program that is active in acquiring ceded lands in Idaho, Oregon, and Washington. In September of 1996 the Nez Perce Tribe signed a Memorandum of Agreement with the BPA. The resulting contract, known as the **Northeast Oregon Wildlife Project**, called for the purchase of approximately 16,500 acres

Wolves are being introduced again into Idaho wilderness areas. (Photo courtesy of Nez Perce Tribe Wildlife Department.)

of wildlife habitat. The general objective of the project is to purchase and manage canyon grasslands and their habitats to benefit wildlife as partial mitigation for construction of the four Lower Snake River Dams. An estimated 9,669 habitat units (HUs) protected under this contract will be credited to BPA for habitat permanently dedicated to wildlife and wildlife mitigation. At the time of this writing, the project contains 15,359 acres of low elevation habitat within and adjacent to the Joseph Creek watershed in northeastern Oregon. Approximately 14.6 miles of perennial streams are being managed to improve riparian habitat conditions to benefit wildlife and Endangered Species Act-listed Snake River steelhead.

United States Fish and Wildlife Service

In 1995, the United States Fish and Wildlife Service (USFWS) entered into a cooperative agreement with the Nez Perce Tribe to recover and manage wolves in Idaho. The Tribe completed, and the USFWS approved, the Nez Perce Tribal Gray Wolf Recovery and Management Plan for Idaho. This plan operates within the broad guidelines set forth in the Final Environmental Impact Statement and Final Rule. The plan is the umbrella document that directs recovery activities in Idaho.

The goal of the **Wolf Recovery Program** is to restore a self-sustaining population of gray wolves to Idaho by maintaining a minimum of 10 breeding pairs for three consecutive years, thereby contributing to the delisting of wolves throughout the northern Rocky Mountains. By integrating four key program elements (monitoring, management and control, information and education, and research), wolf recovery in Idaho employs an effective team approach: the Nez Perce Tribe, federal and state agencies, regional universities, local governments, private organizations, and individuals all work together toward a common goal.

The United States Fish and Wildlife Service and the Nez Perce Tribe also have a Memorandum of Agreement describing production of coho salmon by the Tribe at the USFWS Administration Facility, Dworshak National Fish Hatchery.

Environmental Protection Agency

The Nez Perce Tribe works with the Environmental Protection Agency (EPA) in many different areas. We have applied for and received grants from this agency to conduct various kinds of work. One of our most notable activities is the Nez Perce Tribe's **Air Quality Program**. The Tribe currently administers two air quality projects. One project, begun in 1998, looks at air quality monitoring and data gathering, education and outreach, health effects, and capacity building. The other project is a cooperative agreement between EPA and the Tribe to run a pilot smoke management plan on the reservation for agricultural burning in coordination with the State of Idaho's smoke plan. We also work with the Coeur d' Alene Tribe on a project with the University of Idaho and regional growers on the two reservations to develop alternative Kentucky Bluegrass crop management systems that reduce or eliminate the need for burning.

The Nez Perce Tribe also works with EPA on several programs funded through the Clean Water Act. The Tribe's **Water Resources Division**, for example, uses EPA funding to monitor water quality at 48 sites on the Reservation for baseline data collection, long term assessment, pollution detection, and total maximum daily load development.

The Nez Perce Tribe also works with EPA to implement the **Non-Point Source Program** to restore and improve watersheds. Through this program, the Tribe coordinates with various inter-tribal departments, other local land management agencies, and private landowners on restoration projects. Examples of successful restoration projects include riparian corridor plantings using native tree and shrub species, road stabilization, culvert replacement, campground nutrient management, horse barn cleanup, protective fencing, and soil stabilization. In addition, the Nez Perce Tribe works with the EPA and other federal agencies on various projects, including mine reclamations, point source discharge permits, confined animal feeding operations, and underground storage tanks.

Nez Perce Air Monitoring Station near Kamiah, Idaho. (Photo courtesy of Jennifer Williams.)

Nez Perce Air Monitoring Station near Kamiah, Idaho. (Photo courtesy of Jennifer Williams.)

NEZ PERCE AND THE

U.S. DEPARTMENT OF ENERGY RELATIONSHIP

In the Indian World, it is known that when you take something from the environment, it must be replaced to maintain balance and order. At Hanford, what was taken away was all that was natural and the replacements were things synthetic, artificial, and in all ways "fake." Hanford has taken away our traditional foods. Now we must use grocery stores. It has polluted the air and contaminated the river and groundwater, which affects our health and destroys the fish and animals. We must remember that the Creator gave us our Mother Earth that provides food, one air that we breathe for life, one water to nourish our body, animal and plant life. We must continue as caretakers of the earth, or life will surely end soon.

J. Herman Reuben

The Nez Perce have a centuries long history of resource utilization in the Columbia Basin, including use of the present day Hanford Site. In the 1940s the Hanford Site hosted the original location of the Manhattan Project. The Manhattan Project was responsible for the first full-scale production of weapons grade plutonium that was used to end World War II with the first use of atomic bombs.

Nez Perce Treaty rights extend to natural resources in the Hanford Reach of the Columbia River. That very special stretch of the Columbia River is one of the Tribe's "usual and accustomed" places as stipulated in the Treaty of 1855 and provides a basis for the Nez Perce Tribe's relationship with the United States Department of Energy.

The Environmental Restoration and Waste Management Program (ERWM) is a part of the Nez Perce Tribe's Department of Natural Resources. ERWM facilitates the Tribe's participation in and monitoring of all relevant activities at the U.S. Department of Energy (DOE) Hanford Site. Furthermore, ERWM is the only organization that represents the interests of Idaho at Hanford. ERWM's staff provides oversight and participation in the cleanup and restoration of the Hanford Site. ERWM's involvement at Hanford protects treaty rights as well as both cultural and natural resources.

The Nez Perce ERWM was formed in 1992 to review regulatory documents and to suggest remediation strategies in a number of areas.

Hanford Reach of the Columbia River. (Photo courtesy of The Nature Conservancy.)

ERWM works with agencies such as the United States Environmental Protection Agency and Washington Department of Ecology on hazardous waste and on monitoring projects and health concerns that affect reserved treaty rights at usual and accustomed places and on the Nez Perce Reservation. ERWM is firmly committed to educating tribal members and the reservation community about its (and DOE's) activities at Hanford. This book is one way of doing that.

The ERWM monitors and participates in Hanford environmental restoration and waste management activities by reviewing and analyzing Hanford operations to identify the impacts such operations will have on the environment and upon Nez Perce Treaty rights. The program works to institutionalize Nez Perce involvement in DOE decision-making, in federal compliance with trust responsibility, in protection of treaty rights and privileges, in protection of cultural resources, and in implementation of the DOE Indian policy. ERWM's primary goal, however, is to stop further degradation of the Columbia River Ecosystem and native shrub-steppe habitat. Participation in environmental surveillance and oversight programs enables ERWM to protect treaty rights and to advise DOE and the Tribal public of the efficacy of such programs.

As Indian people, we value that area known as the Hanford Reach. It is a sacred area not only because it is the only place left [on the Columbia River] where salmon still spawn naturally, but it is a place where those fish go to die.

Arthur Taylor, Jr.

NATIONAL PARK SERVICE

I think some of the most important issues relative to the Hanford Reach are the human remains and artifacts that are still there. The erosion of the White Bluffs and also at Locke Island has been directly responsible for exposing many of the artifacts that were previously buried. I think the tribes should be allowed to commemorate, honor, and memorialize anything that is found there and that whatever is found there needs to be left there. We need to get away from that mentality that says, 'It's an archeological find or a dig and therefore we need to take everything and put it in a museum somewhere.' Those artifacts do not belong in a museum. They belong in the earth where they were placed and where they are supposed to remain. When you start doing things like that, you are breaking that circle, and that cycle that is so important for future generations.

Carla HighEagle

The Nez Perce Tribe has an active and ongoing relationship with the Nez Perce National Historical Park whose headquarters and visitor center are located on the reservation near Lapwai. The National Park Service preserves unimpaired the natural and cultural resources and values of the national park system for the enjoyment, education, and inspiration of this and future generations. The Park Service cooperates with partners to extend the benefits of natural and cultural resource conservation and outdoor recreation throughout this country and the world. The Park Service also works with the Nez Perce Tribe to host speakers and presentations. In 1996, the Nez Perce Historical Park presented a three-part seminar on the Nez Perce Treaties led by Professor Dennis Colson of the University of Idaho School of Law. This seminar was presented at a controversial and difficult time when the North Central Idaho Jurisdictional Alliance sought to dismantle tribal sovereignty.

The Park maintains an important photo archive and library often utilized by tribal members. The Park seeks to preserve many other treasures and resources of tangible and intangible nature. For example, the Park Service played a crucial role in acquiring the Spalding-Allen Collection of Nez Perce items for the Nez Perce Tribe. Below is a short history of that purchase.

Footwear from Spalding Allen collection. (Photo courtesy of Nez Perce National Historical Park.)

THE SPALDING-ALLEN COLLECTION

In 1847 the Reverend Henry Spalding sent about two dozen Nez Perce items that he had obtained by barter to his friend Dudley Allen in Ohio who supported the mission. A small portion of the many items he collected included such things as women's dresses, men's leggins, a child's cradle, moccasins, baskets, conhusk bags, hats, a whip, a saddle, and hair cords. These items Dudley Allen kept at his home in Oberlin, Ohio, for twenty years, but in 1893 he donated them to Oberlin College. Oberlin College subsequently loaned the items to the Ohio Historical Society in 1942. The Ohio Historical Society gained ownership of the items in 1980, and in that same year an agreement was reached with the Nez Perce National Historical Park for the items to be displayed at the Park next to the Clearwater River. In 1992, however, the Historical Society requested that the items be returned. This request led to many discussions, but finally an agreement was reached in 1995 with the Historical Society and the Nez Perce Tribe whereby the Nez Perce Tribe would be allowed to purchase the items. The Spalding-Allen Collection was officially purchased and returned to the Tribe in May of 1996. The collection is now on loan to and displayed at the Nez Perce National Historical Park.

NEZ PERCE TRIBE STRATEGIC PLAN

The Nez Perce Strategic Plan is a comprehensive plan that will allow departments to better integrate their priorities with those of the tribe's leadership. It is an opportunity for the tribe to restructure tribal programs based upon the priorities of the tribe.

The goal of the Nez Perce Strategic Plan is to effectively serve and to effectively protect the present and future interests of the Nez Perce People. It is a planning process for tribal leaders

1. to create a vision for the future
2. to identify obstacles and contradictions
3. to identify strategic directions and
4. to develop time-specific implementation steps.

The Nez Perce Strategic Plan was envisioned to give the Tribe a mechanism with which we can, in so far as possible, accurately gauge our development and growth in three primary areas:

1. improving the Nez Perce way of life
2. exercising and protecting Nez Perce sovereignty and
3. developing and improving our governmental services.

The planning process involves elected officials, top tribal management, and key representatives from tribal enterprises. Our mission statement will be integrated into the various tribal departments and will clarify the various roles within the organizational structure, teach and educate our staff and tribal members about programs, and improve our working relationships with each other.

Some of the values that we hold sacred are expressed in our Strategic Plan. Core values in the plan that are discussed below include treaty rights, culture, elders, family, education, empowerment, equality, life, language, and wellness.

TREATY RIGHTS

The old treaty has never been correctly reported.

Chief Joseph, the Younger, 1879

The Nez Perce reserved, within our treaties, certain aboriginal rights that were and are crucial to our continued existence as a people. The treaties also provided a designation of our aboriginal territories. They provided us with the continuing right to choose our own leaders, the right to utilize our usual and accustomed fishing, hunting, and gathering places, the right to use the springs and fountains, the right to pasture animals. These are a few of the rights our people reserved within the Treaty of 1855. There are, of course, other aboriginal rights that we, as Nez Perce people retain and maintain, rights that go unmentioned in the treaties: our right, for example, to follow the religion of our forefathers or our right to speak our own language. Again, we believe it worth repeating that the treaties did not grant us our rights. The treaties were, however, a reservation (and a kind of declaration) of rights that we, the Nez Perce people, already held sacred. We will continue to defend our right to preserve who we are and what we hold sacred.

LOVE FOR CHILDREN, ELDERS, AND FAMILY

The purpose of tradition is to ensure the Tribe's future through its children. By hearing our literature, our stories, our legends, our history, and by watching and dancing and singing and drumming, our children have always learned to honor and respect their proper relationships with other people and with their environment. Among many other things, they learned to be good listeners, careful and accurate and conscientious observers, and to develop and practice patience. Although fewer elders today still tell our traditional Coyote stories, all our elders nevertheless pass on their riches in the family stories they relate and through their extended family relationships, providing our young people with steady and continuing nourishment.

Many tribal families today continue to formally celebrate the achievements of our young people. These celebrations take various forms that include name giving, first kill, and first root-digging ceremonies held by families at special times throughout the year. We also hold community celebrations to honor achievements of our young people by welcoming new births, honoring educational achievements, accomplishments in sports, and other activities. These celebrations help to combine our historic culture with the contemporary world in which our youngsters must be able to excel. Tribal elders encourage positive and loving relationships between parents and their children. The whole Nez Perce community recognizes a child's growth and development. It is often extended family—aunts, uncles, cousins, nieces, and nephews—who assist in the child's development of particular gathering, hunting, or fishing skills.

EDUCATION, EMPOWERMENT, AND SELF-SUFFICIENCY

The education of our people was important to those who negotiated the treaties in 1855 and 1863. Our elders understood the importance of education even prior to the treaties when the sons of various chiefs were sent to the Red River School at Fort Vancouver in the 1830s. Our valuing of education carries forward with each generation.

The Tribe earnestly endeavors to combine science and culture by instituting a circle of learning. We established this circle to provide students with contemporary scientific facts and contemporary knowledge while concurrently providing them with confirmation of the Nez Perce value system. Our goal of self-sufficiency and self-empowerment is tied to our continuing education.

EQUALITY, FAIRNESS, AND INTEGRITY

It is through respect that we value equality, fairness, and integrity. The Nez Perce way of life inevitably creates various roles and responsibilities for our people. We respect and value the equality of the roles within

My friends are very important to me because if I didn't have good friends, I'd do bad things. I need to hang with good friends.

Julian Bronson, 16

Probably the most fun from my growing up and living with my grandmother, she did a lot of things with her grandchildren. She would always take us to dig roots, and when you dig with elders, she would take the best lunch.

Loretta Halfmoon

I have several strengths in my life: God, my parents, my leaders, and my peers. God and my culture because I'm a dancer and a drummer. I enjoy activities like sports that keep me active in the gym. Several things are important to me: my mom, sports, and everything like that. School basketball is something you can look forward to and not to get into trouble. I'd like to stay out of trouble.

Tyler HighEagle, 13

A Nez Perce Tribal Youth Council has recently been reestablished. The Tribe issued a proclamation declaring the Year 2000 as youth Leadership Development Year. If youth are to become our leaders of tomorrow, they must be provided the opportunities to train today. I believe that we must teach our children to become good decision makers and strong leaders, because one day, they will be making decisions for me in my old age.

Simone Wilson

I don't think it's right, the way people are selling our roots and things now. They have taken over the lands and where we get our roots. Some places you can't even go onto the lands. Used to be when we were all taking our roots and stuff, we were all strong and we didn't eat all these soft, sweet foods we eat today.

Gladys Allen

our families, our communities, and our leadership. Our native religion teaches us that all life is equal, all life is sacred. No one person and no one being is a "higher" member of creation than the other. Each has a specific purpose or role as envisioned by the Creator.

Today, we must strive long and hard to maintain equality, fairness, and integrity in our dealings with all other people wherever they are. Unfortunately, some segments of non-Indian society on the reservation view the Tribe and our government as less than equals. We, however, nevertheless maintain our status as equals and will continue to demonstrate our equality in our dealings with other governments.

THE GIFT OF LIFE

Our young people learn that when the taking of a life is necessary, as in hunting, fishing, or food gathering, a special prayer is offered to thank the Creator for this life. In that prayer we promise the nourishment provided by that life will be put to good use. We value the sacrifice of that life so we can continue to exist. We are taught never to take more than we need and never to waste food that has been provided for our use.

Our elders remind us to make good use of this life we have on earth, and to live in a way that shows respect and honor for those whose lives

Mae Taylor, Nez Perce tribal elder. (Photo courtesy of Dan Landeen.)

we represent within our families and communities. This view, of course, is not unique to Nez Perce culture, but it is nonetheless an important and vital part of who we are as Nez Perce people.

NEZ PERCE LANGUAGE

Through the perseverance of our elders, our language—once in real danger of being lost forever—has been preserved, and it is once more becoming increasingly important to the cultural identity of our people. Our language is a source of pride, a source of connection to our past, and a way of communicating that helps us understand and enlarge the meaning of the stories passed down to each generation through our oral (and now our written) traditions. Some of our Nez Perce words have no English equivalents and therefore no accurate translation. To understand the meaning of some of the lessons in our oral literature, including our legends and stories, we all need to learn our language. By learning our native tongue, we can unlock the doors of cultural knowledge that only our native language itself can fully explain.

Many of our place names are tied to characteristics of the physical site or to important events that took place there (or both). A thorough knowledge of our language is essential to a deeper understanding of our culture, our history, and our environment. We invite non-Indians to learn our language as well.

My uncle Irvin said, "Never forget your people, never forget your family, and never forget where you came from."

Anthony Johnson

WELLNESS AND HOLISTIC HEALTH

Long ago our ancestors understood the medicinal values of plants and how to use these plants to treat particular illnesses. This knowledge, still practiced by a few, was based on being in balance and harmony with oneself and the environment. Of course, our tribal healers could not cure the various epidemics and exotic diseases imported into our country by non-Indians. Suffering, panic, and fear of these diseases spread across our homeland. Because of the very real threats brought to us by introduced diseases, our ancestral tribal leaders expressly demanded the inclusion of a skilled and competent non-Indian physician and health care provider for our people if the treaties were to be signed and accepted.

Nez Perce children. (Photo courtesy of Nez Perce National Historical Park.)

The practice of what is now commonly referred to as "holistic health" was fundamental to our traditional religious beliefs in living in balance and harmony. The practice of holistic health treatment is now part of

The Soup Dance is a very powerful vehicle to show our children that there were people who cared about our wounded. The dancers go out there and dance around the soup. We're bringing the veterans back in to our village and letting them know that we love them and care for them, and I think that's why I danced today here at Mah-Ta-Lyma Pow Wow. When I dance I have a lot of love and happiness in my heart. Sometimes I feel sadness when I dance because I get a really powerful feeling that a lot of veterans didn't make it through the wars and I can just feel their spirits touching me, and it's like I was carrying them back home.

Anthony HighEagle Jr.

the tribal programs designed for the disease prevention and treatment of tribal members. Programs are now being designed that recognize the various roles of family members in building healthy families. Our treatment plans must look at the mental, spiritual, physical, and social aspects of an individual. This old "new" approach will increase our chances of healing our people and keeping them healthy.

During the treaty making time, our leaders were also very concerned about keeping alcohol off the reservation. So great, in fact, was their concern for the problems associated with the misuse of alcohol and the additional problems it could create for our tribe that our leaders insisted that a written prohibition against alcohol be included as a part of the treaties of 1855 and 1863 and as a part of the 1893 Agreement.

AMERICAN ARMED FORCES

Indian people served in the armed forces even before they were granted citizenship in 1924. In 1917 and 1918, over 10,000 American Indians enlisted in the armed services to serve in World War I. More than 44,000 American Indians served from 1941-1945 in both European and Pacific theaters of war.

Veterans at memorial service celebration at Spalding in 2000. (Photo courtesy of Rebecca Williams.)

Nez Perce tribal members take their United States citizenship seriously and have a long history of supporting the government during its involvement in wars it has fought throughout the world. Well over 300 Nez Perce tribal members (both men and women) have served in the armed forces in World War I, World War II, Korean War, Vietnam War, and the Gulf War. Many tribal veterans have been paratroopers. Many tribal members today are also serving in various branches of the armed services. Each year the Tribe celebrates and honors those veterans who have represented the Tribe and their country.

CURRENT CHALLENGES TO THE

NEZ PERCE TRIBE TREATY RIGHTS

Good relationships with federal agencies, state agencies, and local governments are a vital part of the Nez Perce Tribe's efforts to improve the lives of our people. Over the very short span of time that our Nez Perce governments and our people have interacted with newer governments, the Tribe has been subjected to countless misunderstandings, broken promises, and bad faith negotiations. Rebuilding relationships will serve all parties in a positive way. As our natural resources dwindle and our ecosystems continue to deteriorate and decline, it is especially important that good relationships grow even stronger and continue so that global assistance can be aimed at these growing problems.

Solid, mutually respectful relationships based on sovereignty are the foundation for the future. The Nez Perce Tribe will continue to bring our culture, our traditions, and our expertise to the table while addressing the challenging issues facing Indian people today, as well as those issues that may arise in the future. We have survived by adapting to change in our own way. As we look forward now, into the times that are yet to be, we therefore reflect back on the past to guide us on our journey.

In 1855, the Nez Perce Tribe reserved, for future generations, rights that were essential to the Tribe's culture, beliefs, economy, and way of life. Today, the Nez Perce Tribe has taken a leadership role in restoring the natural resources that are so critical to being *Niimiipuu*. The Tribe's undertook management of gray wolves in Idaho, and the Tribe's success is evident: gray wolves are close to being delisted under the federal Endangered Species Act. The Tribe's deep commitment to salmon recovery is evident in its habitat restoration and supplementation activities, as well as in its constant advocacy. The Tribe's positions

As the health of the water and the fish have declined, so has the health and welfare of our people declined with increased diabetes, alcoholism, and things like this; they have taken away those things that are so dear to us the clean water and healthy fish runs.…My father and his brother, Norman Holt, who passed on, used to go to a place called the Blue Hole on the Imnaha River. It was a very deep and beautiful hole, and they used to go there every year to fish for salmon, summer Chinook, what we called "June Hogs." And as he became a young man in his twenties right after Lower Granite Dam went in, he saw the decline of those fish. Him and his brother. So one day, he and his brother, being conservationists at heart, told themselves that they would not return to that fishing hole until the salmon came back in healthy runs again. And they never went back since. So to me that act represents the impacts that the dams have had on our salmon. It shows a reflection of me, and why the dams need to come out. That to me is another reason why the spiritual and physical aspects and strengths of our people are going away.

James Holt

on natural resource management continue to reaffirm that the Tribe has always been here and does not intend to go anywhere. Thus, in advocating for breaching the lower Snake River dams to rebuild salmon runs, the Tribe is also supporting investments in the local communities that would be affected by that decision. Despite the Tribe's leadership, many challenges remain to fulfill the rights that the Tribe reserved and that the United States secured to the Tribe.

Lewis and Clark, in passing through Nez Perce Country, recorded in their journals runs of salmon that they could only describe as "nearly inexhaustible." Yet today, every species of salmon and steelhead returning to the Tribe's usual and accustomed fishing places in Nez Perce Country is either extinct (Snake River coho), endangered (Snake River sockeye) or threatened (Snake River spring, summer, and fall chinook; Snake River steelhead). A recent report of tribal circumstances has documented the high status of unemployment, poverty, and other problems among the Nez Perce and other treaty tribes that are directly traceable to destruction of treaty-reserved assets.

The Tribe has long restricted its harvest in hopes that the United States and the States would take actions to restore these salmon runs. Today, much of the salmon is being harvested by the United States, through the operation of the Federal Columbia River Power System, timber, grazing and road construction on Forest Service and Bureau of Land Management lands. This leaves the Tribe's treaty fishermen in nearly the same place they were in the late 1960's—being placed at the end of the line after all other harvest had occurred and being asked to bear the conservation burden.

Will the United States ever honor the promises it made in the treaties? As the Tribe's trustee, will the United States ensure that the Tribe's rights are protected? Will the Nation reciprocate the generosity the Tribe demonstrated in rescuing the struggling Lewis and Clark party 200 years ago by assisting the Nez Perce in restoring resources that are icons of the Pacific Northwest? These are the questions that remain to be answered in the days ahead. It is the fervent hope of the Nez Perce that "great nations, like great men, keep their word."

Otis Halfmoon and Allen Pinkham, Sr. at Whitebird Memorial. (Photo courtesy of Antonio Smith.)

Appendix 1

A Nez Perce Creation Story

The following account is one version of the Nez Perce creation story that explains the origins of geological features as well as the important reciprocal relationships the Creator established between the animals and human beings. It should also be noted that there are several accounts and variations of the Creation story.

A Meeting Between Creator and the Animals

On one of the slopes of the Clearwater River near Lewiston, Idaho, there are a lot of rounded stones going up one of the draws. As you look along the ridgeline there are also other rocks of all different sizes and forms, but most of them are very large. Some of these are referred to by the Nez Perce as the "large animals." They are the remains of the large animals before there were human beings. The Nez Perces have always known that at one time there were large animals that inhabited this country because we find large bones in the ground between Clarkston and Pasco. The Creator called all of these large animals together telling them that there was going to be a great change, and he said that some of them probably wouldn't survive. Many of the animals were late to the meeting that the Creator had called and as a result were turned to stone. So Creator called all the large animal people together and said there was going to be a great change and that he wanted all of the animals to qualify themselves for a new kind of human being that would be coming as a result of this great change. Creator wanted to know who was going to be qualified to help these new human beings when they came because those human beings were going to be naked, and they were going to have a hard time making a living. The Creator said, "I want each one of you to come forward and be qualified to help these new human beings when they come." So all the animals had to come up and be qualified.

The Nez Perce people could describe every animal including the birds, fishes, and insects that they knew of with this story. This is one story that they could relate for days and days to the young people and tell them how they used these species to survive.

So Deer, he comes out and says, "I want to have horns that come up and branch out, and I want to have big ears so I can hear well, and I want a little short tail with a black tip on it. These new human beings when they come can use my horn to make arrows and flint knives, and they can use my hide for clothing to keep warm, and they can use my hooves to make rattles to sing their songs with." So Creator said, "You act the way you want to act, and that's the way you will be," and that deer is what we call mule deer today.

Well, another deer came forward and said, "I don't want to be like that one. I want to have horns that come up a different way and then branch out. I don't like large ears and I want a tail that's longer," and so he described himself how he wanted to be, and he also said that the new human beings could use his body parts and also his brains to help them tan the hides and make them soft and white. That deer was called Blacktail deer. The Creator said, "Okay, you are qualified to help these new human beings when they come."

Another deer came forward and said, "I don't like those horns that come up and branch like the other ones. I want them to come up and go back and go straight up, and I don't like large ears, but I want a long tail that will wave when I run, and it will give warning to others in the woods when I run." That was Whitetail deer, and he also said that the new human beings could use his body parts. Then Moose came forward and said, "I want to be bigger, I want to be black, and I want white feet, and I want my horns to be flat with points on them, and I want to have wide feet so I can wade around in the mud and eat those plants that grow in the water." Moose also said that the new human beings could use his body parts for clothing and food. Then Elk came forth and said, "I don't want to have flat horns like Moose. I want to have horns that come up and branch out and have points." Then he described himself, and Creator said, "Okay, you are qualified."

Then Eagle came forward and said, "I want to fly up high so that I can bring the messages to you from these new human beings, and they can use my feathers for ceremonies and symbols so that they know who the Creator is." Creator said, "Okay, you are qualified." Then Crow came out and said, "I want to be black and I'll be a warning to the other animals in times of danger." So Creator said, "Okay, you are qualified." Then another Crow came out and said, "I don't want to be that small, I want to be bigger, and I want a different sounding voice, but I still want to be black," and that bird was Raven. So Creator said, "Okay, you are qualified." Then another bird came out and said, "I don't want to be all black, I want a long black and white tail, and I'll also be a warning to the people." That bird was Magpie. Then Bee came forward and said, "I'll make honey that is very sweet, and they can use it for food, but I'll sting them to protect what I have." So Bee became qualified. Spider came forward, and he said, "I would like to give these new human beings wisdom. When I make my webs they'll never know how I make the webs, and yet I can catch food. This will tell them that I have something that they can acquire, but it will take a long time for them to learn how to get that wisdom." So Creator let the Spider be qualified.

Salmon and Steelhead came forward and said, "We can help the human beings with our flesh." Salmon said, "When we come up the river we will die, so the human beings will have to catch us before that happens. I'll come up only on certain times of the year, and that's when they'll have to catch me." Then Steelhead said, "I want to come in the wintertime, but I'll give them something special. That will be the glue from my skin. This glue can be used to make bows and spears. I'll be in the water all winter long." So Creator let Steelhead become qualified. Sockeye Salmon came forward and he said, "I don't want to be big like Chinook Salmon and Steelhead, and my flesh will be red because I will eat different foods." Then Trout came forward and he said, "I am going to look like Steelhead, but I am not going to go down to the ocean. I'll just stay here in the waters even in the winter, and if these human beings can find me they can have me for food. But in the wintertime I will be down in the gravel and if they can find me that's where I will be." Then Eel came out and said, "I don't want to look like the Steelhead or Salmon or Trout. I want to be long, and when I rest I want to put my mouth on the rocks. But I'll come up the river every year, and they can use my flesh for food." So this is how the fish became qualified.

The last animal to be qualified was Coyote. Coyote came out, and he couldn't get qualified. He tried to be qualified to do something, but he couldn't do it. You know when you hear Coyote today, he goes yip, yip, yip. He couldn't even talk. When Coyote talks, it sounds like two or three coyotes talking at the same time. So he couldn't get qualified, and finally Creator said that he would take pity on him. He said, "Because you can't get qualified I'll give you special powers. When these new human beings come, you will have all the faults and all of the traits that this new human being will have. That's what you will be able to do, but I'll give you some special powers beyond that. You will be able to transform and change yourself, and you will be able to get out of bad situations in order to save yourself. You will also be able to teach these new human beings many things." Creator said, "I'll make you qualified, but you'll get to be gray. You won't have any other colors." That's the way Coyote was created, and that's how Coyote became qualified to help the new human beings.

About this time Grizzly Bear spoke up and said, "What are we going to do about day and night? I want six months of night and six months of day." Chipmunk perked up and said, "We can't have that. I want one day and one night." So Chipmunk and Grizzly Bear started to argue. Grizzly Bear said that he wanted six months of day and six months of night so he could rest and sleep for half the year and work for the other half of the year. Chipmunk was adamant that there would be one day and one night. Finally, Creator told the two of them to go off to have their argument, and he told them that whoever won the argument would determine the way the new world would be created. So Grizzly Bear and Chipmunk went off and continued arguing.

After a long time, Grizzly Bear started to get tired, and he was trying not to go to sleep but Chipmunk was still going strong. Finally, Grizzly Bear got so tired that he went to sleep. Chipmunk yelled, "I won, I won, there will be one day and one night when those new human beings come." Creator replied, "That's the way it will be from now on, one day and one night." Soon, Grizzly bear awoke and found out from the other animals that he had lost the argument. This made him angry and he started chasing Chipmunk. As Chipmunk was trying to get away, Grizzly Bear put out his claws and scratched Chipmunk on the back, and that is why today the Chipmunk has black and white stripes on his back.

Allen Pinkham (Nez Perce)

Appendix 2

Treaty with the Nez Perces, 1855

rticles of agreement and convention made and concluded at the treaty ground, Camp Stevens, in the Walla-Walla Valley, this eleventh day of June, in the year one thousand eight hundred and fifty-five, by and between Isaac I. Stevens, governor and Superintendent of Indian affairs for the Territory of Washington, and Joel Palmer, Superintendent of Indian affairs for Oregon Territory, on the part of the United States, and the undersigned chiefs, headmen, and delegates of the Nez Perce tribe of Indians occupying lands lying partly in Oregon and partly in Washington Territories, between the Cascade and Bitterroot Mountains, on behalf of, and acting for said tribe, and being duly authorized thereto by them, it being understood that Superintendent Isaac I. Stevens assumes to treat only with those of the above named tribe of Indians residing within the Territory of Washington, and Superintendent Palmer with those residing exclusively in Oregon Territory.

ARTICLE 1. The said Nez Perce tribe of Indians hereby cede, relinquish and convey to the United States all their right, title, and interest in and to the country occupied or claimed by them, bounded and described as follows, to wit: Commencing at the source of the Wo-na-ne-she or southern tributary of the Palouse River; thence down that river to the main Palouse: thence in a southerly direction to the Snake River, at the mouth of the Tucanon River; thence up the Tucanon to its source in the Blue Mountains; thence southerly along the ridge of the Blue Mountains thence to a point on Grand Ronde River, midway between Grand Ronde and the mouth of the Woll-low-how River: thence along the divide between the waters of the Woll-low-how and Powder River; thence to the crossing of Snake River at the mouth of Powder River: thence to the Salmon River, fifty miles above the place known [as] the "crossing of the Salmon River;" thence due north to the summit of the Bitter Root Mountains: thence along the crest of the Bitter Root Mountains to the place of beginning.

ARTICLE 2. There is, however, reserved from the lands above ceded for the use and occupation of the said tribe, and as a general reservation for other friendly tribes and bands of Indians in Washington Territory, not to exceed, the present numbers of the Spokane, Walla-Walla, Cayuse, and Umatilla tribes and bands of Indians, the tract of land included within the following boundaries, to wit: Commencing where the Moh ha-na-she or southern tributary of the Palouse River flows from the spurs of the Bitter Root Mountains; thence down said tributary to the mouth of the Ti-nat-pan-up Creek; thence southerly to the crossing of the Snake River ten miles below the mouth of the Al-po-wa-wi River; thence to the source of the Al-po-wa-wi River in the Blue Mountains; thence along the crest of the Blue Mountains; thence to the crossing of the Grand Ronde River, midway between the Grand Ronde and the mouth of the Woll-low-how River; thence along the divide between the waters of the Woll-low-how and Powder Rivers; thence to the crossing of the Snake River fifteen miles below the mouth of the Powder River; thence to the Salmon River above the crossing; thence by the spurs of the Bitter Root Mountains to the place of beginning.

All which tract shall be set apart, and, so far as necessary, surveyed and marked out for the exclusive use and benefit of said tribe as an Indian reservation; nor shall any white man, excepting those in the employment of the Indian Department, be permitted to reside upon the said reservation without permission of the tribe and the superintendent and agent; and the said tribe agrees to remove to and settle upon the same within one year after the ratification of this treaty. In the mean time it shall be lawful for them to reside upon any ground not in the actual claim and occupation of citizens of the United States, and upon any ground claimed or occupied, if with the permission of the owner or claimant, and guaranteeing, however, the right to all citizens of the United States to enter upon an occupy as settlers any lands not actually occupied and cultivated by said Indians at this time, and not included in the reservation above named. And provided that any substantial improvement heretofore made by any Indian, such as fields enclosed and cultivated, and houses erected upon the lands hereby ceded, and which he may be compelled to abandon in consequence of this treaty, shall be valued under the direction of the President of the United States, and payment made therefore in money, or improvements of an equal value be made for said Indian upon the reservation, and no Indian will be required to abandon the improvements aforesaid now occupied by him, until their value in money or improvements of equal value shall be , furnished him as aforesaid.

ARTICLE 3. And provided that, if necessary for the public convenience, roads may be run through the said reservation, and, on the other hand, the right of way, with free access from the same to the nearest public highway is secured to them, as also the right, in common with citizens of the United States, to travel upon all public highways. The use of the Clear Water and other streams flowing through the reservation is also secured to citizens of the United States for rafting purposes, and as public highways.

The exclusive right of taking fish in all the streams where running through or bordering said reservation is further secured to said Indians; as also the right of taking fish at all usual and accustomed places in common with citizens of the Territory; and of erecting temporary buildings for curing, together with the privilege of hunting, gathering roots and berries, and pasturing their horses and cattle upon open and unclaimed land.

ARTICLE 4. In consideration of the above cession, the United States agree to pay to the said tribe in addition to the goods and provisions distributed to them at the time of signing this treaty, the sum of two hundred thousand dollars, in the following manner, that is to say, sixty thousand dollars, to be expended under the direction of the President of the United States, the first year after the ratification of this treaty, in providing for their removal to the reserve, breaking up and fencing farms, building houses, supplying them with provisions and a suitable outfit, and for such other objects as he may deem necessary and the remainder in annuities, as follows: for the first five years after the ratification of this treaty, ten thousand dollars each year, commencing September 1,1856; for the next five years, eight thousand dollars each year for the next five years, six thousand each year, and for the next five years, four thousand dollars each year.

All which said sums of money shall be applied to the use and benefit of the said Indians, under the direction of the President of the United States, who may from time to time determine, at his discretion upon what beneficial objects to expend the same for them. And the superintendent of Indian affairs or other proper officer, shall each year inform the President of the wishes of the Indians in relation thereto.

ARTICLE 5. The United States further agree to establish at suitable points within said reservation, within one year after the ratification hereof, two schools erecting the necessary buildings, keeping the same in repair, and providing them with furniture, books, and stationery, one of which shall be an agricultural and industrial school, to be located at the agency and to be free to the children of said tribe, and to employ one superintendent of teaching and two teachers; to build two blacksmiths' shops, to one of which shall be attached a tin shop and to the other a gunsmith's shop; one carpenter's shop, one wagon and plough maker's shop, and to keep the same in repair, and furnished with the necessary tools; to employ one superintendent of farming and two farmers, two blacksmiths one tinner, one gunsmith one carpenter, one wagon and plough maker, for the instruction of the Indians in trades, and to assist them in the same; to erect one saw-mill and one flouring-mill, keeping the same in repair, and furnished with the necessary tools and fixtures, and to employ two millers; to erect a hospital, keeping the same in repair, and provided with the necessary medicines and furniture, and to employ a physician; and to erect, keep in repair, and provide with the necessary furniture the buildings required for the accommodation of the said employees. The said buildings and establishments to be maintained and kept in repair as aforesaid, and the employees to be kept in service for the period of twenty years.

And in view of the fact that the head chief of the tribe is expected, and will he called upon, to perform many services of a public character, occupying much of his time, the United States further agrees to pay to the Nez Perce tribe five hundred dollars per year for the term of twenty years, after the ratification hereof, as a salary for such person as the tribe may select to be its head chief. To build for him, at a suitable point on the reservation, a comfortable house, and properly furnished the same, and to plough and fence for his use ten acres of land. The said salary to be paid to, and the said house to be occupied by such head chief so long as he may be elected to that position by his tribe, and no longer.

And all the expenditures and expenses contemplated in this fifth article of this treaty shall be defrayed by the United States, and shall not be deducted from the annuities agreed to be paid to said tribe, nor shall the cost of transporting the goods for the annuity-payments be a charge upon the annuities, but shall be defrayed by the United States.

Article 6. The President may from time to time at his discretion, cause the whole, or such portions of such reservation as he may think proper, to be surveyed into lots, and assign the same to such individuals or families of the said tribe as are willing to avail themselves of the privilege, and will locate on the same as a permanent home, on the same terms and subject to the same regulations as are provided in the sixth article of the treaty with the Omahas in the year 1854, so far as the same may be applicable.

Article 7. The annuities of the aforesaid tribe shall not be taken to pay the debts of individuals.

Article 8. The aforesaid tribe acknowledge their dependence upon the Government of the United States, and promise to be friendly with all citizens thereof, and pledge themselves to commit no depredations on the property of such citizens; and should any one or more of them violate this pledge, and the fact be satisfactorily proved before the agent, the property taken shall be returned, or in default thereof, or if injured or destroyed, compensation may be made by the Government out of the annuities. Nor will they make war on any other tribe except in self-defence, but will submit all matters of difference between them and the other Indians to the Government of the United States, or its agent, for decision, and abide thereby; and if any of the said Indians commit any depredations on any other Indians within the Territory of Washington, the same rule shall prevail as that prescribed in this article in cases of depredations against citizens. And the said tribe agrees not to shelter or conceal offenders against the laws of the United States, but to deliver them up to the authorities for trial.

Article 9. The Nez Perces desire to exclude from their reservation the use of ardent spirits, and to prevent their people from drinking the same; and therefore it is provided that any Indian belonging to said tribe who is guilty of bringing liquor into said reservation, or who drinks liquor, may have his or her proportion of the annuities withheld from him or her for such time as the President may determine.

Article 10. The Nez Perce Indians having expressed in council a desire that William Craig should continue to live with them, he having, uniformly shown himself their friend, it is further agreed that the tract of land now occupied by him, and described in his notice to the register and receiver of the land office of the Territory of Washington, on the fourth day of June last, shall not be considered a part of the reservation provided for in this treaty, except that it shall be subject in common with the lands of the reservation to the operations of the intercourse act.

Article 11. This treaty shall be obligatory upon the contracting parties as soon as the same shall be ratified by the President and Senate of the United States.

In testimony whereof, the said Isaac I. Stevens, governor and superintendent of Indian affairs for the Territory of Washington, and Joel Palmer, superintendent of Indian affairs for Oregon Territory, and the chiefs, headmen, and delegates of the aforesaid Nez Perce tribe of Indians, have hereunto set their hands and seals, at the place, and on the day and year herein before written.

Isaac I. Stevens,   [L.S.]
Governor and Superintendent Washington Territory.
Joel Palmer,   [L.S.]
Superintendent Indian Affairs.

Aleiya, or Lawyer, Head-chief of the Nez Perces	[L.S.]	Tippelanecbupooh, his x mark.	[L.S.]
		Hah-hah-stilpilp, his x mark.	[L.S.]
Appushwa-hite, or Looking-glass, his x mark.	[L.S.]	Cool-cool-shua-nin, his x mark.	[L.S.]
		Silish, his x mark.	[L.S.]
Joseph, his x mark.	[L.S.]	Toh-toh-molewit, his x mark.	[L.S.]
James, his x mark.	[L.S.]	Tuky-in-lik-it, his x mark.	[L.S.]
Red Wolf, his x mark.	[L.S.]	Te-hole-hole-soot, his x mark.	[L.S.]
Timothy, his x mark.	[L.S.]	Ish-coh-tim, his x mark.	[L.S.]
U-ute-sin-male-cun, his x mark.	[L.S.]	Wee-as-cus, his x mark.	[L.S.]
Spotted Eage, his x mark.	[L.S.]	Hah-hah-stoore-tee, his x mark.	[L.S.]
Stoop-toop-nin or Cut-hair, his x mark.	[L.S.]	Eee-maht-sin-pooh, his x mark.	[L.S.]
Tah-moh-moh-kin, his x mark.	[L.S.]	Tow-wish-au-il-pilp, his x mark.	[L.S.]
Speaking Eagle, his x mark.	[L.S.]	Kay-kay-mass, his x mark.	[L.S.]
Wat-ti-wat-ti-wah-hi, his x mark.	[L.S.]	Kole-kole-til-ky, his x mark.	[L.S.]
Howh-no-tah-kun, his x mark.	[L.S.]	In-mat-tute-kah-ky, his x mark.	[L.S.]
Tow-wish-wane, his x mark.	[L.S.]	Moh-see-chee, his x mark.	[L.S.]
Wahpt-tah-shooshe, his x mark.	[L.S.]	George, his x mark.	[L.S.]
Bead Necklace, his x mark.	[L.S.]	Nicke-el-it-may-ho, his x mark.	[L.S.]
Koos-koos-tas-kut, his x mark.	[L.S.]	Say-i-ee-ouse, his x mark.	[L.S.]
Levi, his x mark.	[L.S.]	Wis-tasse-cut, his x mark.	[L.S.]
Pee-oo-pe-whi-hi, his x mark.	[L.S.]	Ky-ky-soo-te-lum, his x mark.	[L.S.]
Pee-oo-pee-iecteim, his x mark.	[L.S.]	Ko-ko-whay-nee, his x mark.	[L.S.]
Pee-poome-kah, his x mark.	[L.S.]	Kwin-to-kow, his x mark.	[L.S.]
Hah-hah-still-at-me, his x mark.	[L.S.]	Pee-wee-au-ap-tah, his x mark.	[L.S.]
Wee-yoke-sin-ate, his x mark.	[L.S.]	Wee-at-tenat-il-pilp, his x mark.	[L.S.]
Wee-ah-ki, his x mark.	[L.S.]	Pee-oo-pee-u-il-pilp, his x mark.	[L.S.]
Necalahtsin, his x mark.	[L.S.]	Wah-tass-tum-mannee, his x mark.	[L.S.]
Suck-on-tie, his x mark.	[L.S.]	Tu-wee-si-ce, his x mark.	[L.S.]
Ip-nat-tam-moose, his x mark.	[L.S.]	Lu-ee-sin-kah-koose-sin, his x mark.	[L.S.]
Jason, his x mark.	[L.S.]	Hah-tal-ee-kin, his x mark.	[L.S.]

Appendix 3

Treaty with the Nez Perces, 1863

Articles of agreement made and concluded at the Council Ground, in the valley of the Lapwai, W. T., on the ninth day of June, one thousand Eight hundred and sixty-three, between the United States of America, by C. H. Hale, superintendent of Indian Affairs, and Charles Hutchins and S. D. Howe, U. S. Indian agents, for the Territory of Washington, acting on the part and in behalf of the United States, and the Nez Perce Indians, by the chiefs, headmen, and delegates of said tribe, such articles being supplementary and amendatory to the treaty made between the United States and said tribe on the 11th day of June, 1855.

ARTICLE 1. The said Nez Perce tribe agree to relinquish, and do hereby relinquish, to the United States the lands heretofore reserved for the use and occupation of the said tribe, saving and excepting so much thereof as is described in article II for a new reservation.

ARTICLE 2. The United States agree to reserve for a home, and for the sole use and occupation of said tribe, the tract of land included within the following boundaries, to wit: Commencing at the N.E. corner of Lake Wa-ha, and running thence, northerly, to a point on the north bank of the Clearwater River, three miles below the mouth of the Lapwai, thence down the north bank of the Clearwater to the mouth of the Hatwai creek; thence, due north, to a point seven miles distant; thence, eastwardly, to a point on the north fork of the Clearwater, seven miles distant from its mouth; thence to a point on Oro Fino Creek, five miles above its mouth; thence to a point on the north fork of the south fork of the Clearwater, five miles above its mouth; thence to a point on the south fork of the Clearwater, one mile above the bridge, on the road leading to Elk City, (so as to include all the Indian farms within the forks;) thence in a straight line, westwardly, to the place of beginning.

All of which tract shall be set apart, and the above-described boundaries shall be surveyed and marked out for the exclusive use and benefit of said tribe as an Indian reservation, nor shall any white man, excepting those in the employment of the Indian department, be permitted to reside upon the said reservation without permission of the tribe and the superintendent and agent; and the said tribe agrees that so soon after the United States shall make the necessary provision for fulfilling the stipulations of this instrument as they can conveniently arrange their affairs, and not to exceed one year from its ratification, they will vacate the country hereby relinquished, and remove to and settle upon the lands herein reserved for them, (except as may be hereinafter provided.) In the mean time it shall be lawful for them to reside upon any ground now occupied or under cultivation by said Indians at this time, and not included in the reservation above named. And it is provided, that any substantial improvement heretofore made by any Indian, such as fields enclosed and cultivated, or houses erected upon the lands hereby relinquished, and which he may be compelled to abandon in consequence of this treaty, shall be valued under the direction of the President of the United States, and payment therefore shall be made in stock or in improvements of an equal value for said Indian upon the lot which may be assigned to him within the bounds of the reservation, as he may choose, and no Indian will be required to abandon the improvements aforesaid, now occupied by him, until said payment or improvement shall have been made. And it is further provided, that if any Indian living on any of the land hereby relinquished should prefer to sell his improvements to any white man, being a loyal citizen of the United States, prior to the same being valued as aforesaid, he shall be allowed so to do, but the sale or transfer of said improvements shall be made in the presence of, and with the consent and approval of, the agent or superintendent, by whom a certificate of sale shall be issued to the party purchasing, which shall set forth the amount of the consideration in kind. Before the issue of said certificate, the agent or superintendent shall be satisfied that a valuable consideration is paid, and that the party purchasing is of undoubted loyalty to the United States government. No settlement or claim made upon the improved lands of any Indian will be permitted, except as herein provided, prior to the time specified for their removal. Any sale or transfer thus made shall be in the stead of payment for improvements from the United States.

ARTICLE 3. The President shall, immediately after the ratification of this treaty, cause the boundary lines to be surveyed, and properly marked and established; after which, so much of the lands hereby reserved as may be suitable for cultivation shall be surveyed into lots of twenty acres each, and every male person of the tribe who shall have attained the age of twenty-one years, or is the head of a family, shall have the privilege of locating upon one lot as a permanent home for such person, and the lands so surveyed shall be allotted under such rules and regulations as the President shall prescribe, having such reference to their settlement as may secure adjoining each other the location of the different families pertaining to each band, so far as the same may be practicable. Such rules and regulations shall be prescribed by the President, or under his direction, as will insure to the family, in case of the death of the head thereof, the possession and enjoyment of such permanent home, and the improvements thereon. When the assignments as above shall have been completed, certificates shall be issued by the Commissioner of Indian Affairs, or under his direction, for the tracts assigned in severalty, specifying the names of the individuals to whom they have been assigned respectively, and that said tracts are set apart for the perpetual and exclusive use and benefit of such assignees and their heirs. Until otherwise provided by law, such tracts shall be exempt from levy, taxation, or sale, and shall be alienable in fee, or leased, or otherwise disposed of, only to the United States, or to persons then being members of the Nez Perce tribe, and of Indian blood, with the permission of the President, and under such regulations as the Secretary of the Interior or the Commissioner of Indian Affairs shall prescribe; and if any such person or family shall at any time neglect or refuse to occupy and till a portion of the land so assigned, and on which they have located, or shall rove from place to place, the President may cancel the assignment, and may also withhold from such person or family their proportion of the annuities or other payments due them until they shall have returned to such permanent home, and resumed the pursuits of industry; and in default of their return, the tract may be declared abandoned, and thereafter assigned to some other person or family of such tribe. The residue of the land hereby reserved shall be held in common for pasturage for the sole use and benefit of the Indians: Provided, however, That from time to time, as members of the tribe may come upon the reservation, or may become of proper age, after the expiration of the time of one year after the ratification of this treaty, as aforesaid, and claim the privileges granted under this article, lots may be assigned from the lands thus held in common, where-ever the same may be suitable for cultivation. No State or territorial legislature shall remove the restriction herein provided for, without the consent of Congress, and no State or territorial law to that end shall be deemed valid until the same has been specially submitted to Congress for its approval.

Article 4. In consideration of the relinquishment herein made the United States agree to pay to the said tribe, in addition to the annuities provided by the treaty of June 11th, 1855, and the goods and provisions distributed to them at the time of signing this treaty, the sum of two hundred and sixty-two thousand and five hundred dollars, in manner following, to wit:

First. One hundred and fifty thousand dollars, to enable the Indians to remove and locate upon the reservation, to be expended in the ploughing of land, and the fencing of the several lots, which may be assigned to those individual members of the tribe who will accept the same in accordance with the provisions of the preceding article, which said sum shall be divided into four annual installments, as follows: For the first year after the ratification of this treaty, seventy thousand dollars; for the second year, forty thousand dollars; for the third year, twenty-five thousand dollars; and for the fourth year, fifteen thousand dollars.

Second. Fifty thousand dollars to be paid the first year after the ratification of this treaty in agricultural implements, to include wagons or carts, harness, and cattle, sheep, or other stock, as may be deemed most beneficial by the superintendent of Indian affairs, or agent, after ascertaining the wishes of the Indians in relation thereto.

Third. Ten thousand dollars for the erection of a saw and flouring mill, to be located at Kamia, the same to be erected within one year after the ratification hereof.

Fourth. Fifty thousand dollars for the boarding and clothing of the children who shall attend the schools, in accordance with such rules or regulations as the Commissioner of Indian Affairs may prescribe, providing the schools and boarding-houses with necessary furniture, the purchase of necessary wagons, teams, agricultural implements, tools, &c., for their use, and for the fencing of such lands as may be needed for gardening and farming purposes, for the use and benefit of the schools, to be expended as follows: The first year after the ratification of this treaty six thousand dollars; for the next fourteen years, three thousand dollars each year; and for the succeeding year, being the sixteenth and last installment, two thousand dollars.

Fifth. A further sum of two thousand five hundred dollars shall be paid within one year after the ratification hereof, to enable the Indians to build two churches, one of which is to be located at some suitable point on the Kamia, and the other on the Lapwai.

Article 5. The United States further agree, that in addition to a head chief the tribe shall elect two subordinate chiefs, who shall assist him in the performance of his public services, and each subordinate chief shall have the same amount of land ploughed and fenced, with comfortable house and necessary furniture, and to whom the same salary shall be paid as is already provided for the head chief in art. 5th of the treaty of June 11th, 1855, the salary to be paid and the houses and land to be occupied during the same period and under like restrictions as therein mentioned.

And for the purpose of enabling the agent to erect said buildings, and to plough and fence the land, as well as to procure the necessary furniture, and to complete and furnish the house, &c., of the head chief, as heretofore provided, there shall be appropriated, to be expended within the first year after the ratification hereof, the sum of two thousand five hundred dollars.

And inasmuch as several of the provisions of said art. 5th of the treaty of June 11th, 1855, pertaining to the erection of school-houses, hospital, shops, necessary buildings for employees and for the agency, as well as providing the same with necessary furniture, tools, &c., have not yet been complied with, it is hereby stipulated that there shall be appropriated, to be expended for the purposes herein specified during the first year after the ratification hereof, the following sums, to wit:

First. Ten thousand dollars for the erection of the two schools, including boarding-houses and the necessary outbuildings; said schools to be conducted on the manual-labor system as far as practicable.

Second. Twelve hundred dollars for the erection of the hospital, and providing the necessary furniture for the same.

Third. Two thousand dollars for the erection of a blacksmith's shop, to be located at Kamiah, to aid in the completion of the smith's shop at the agency, and to purchase the necessary tools, iron, steel etc.; and to keep the same in repair and properly stocked with necessary tools and materials, there shall be appropriated thereafter, for the fifteen years next succeeding, the sum of five hundred dollars each year.

Fourth. Three thousand dollars for erection of houses for employees, repairs of mills, shops, etc., and providing necessary furniture, tools, and materials. For the same purpose, and to procure from year to year the necessary articles—that is to say, saw-logs, nails, glass, hardware, etc.—there shall be appropriated thereafter, for the twelve years next succeeding, the sum of two thousand dollars each year; and for the next three years, one thousand dollars each year.

And it is further agreed that the United States shall employ, in addition to those already mentioned in art. 5th of the treaty of June 11th, 1855, two matrons to take charge of the boarding -schools, two assistant teachers, one farmer, one carpenter, and two millers.

All the expenditures and expenses contemplated in this treaty, and not otherwise provided for, shall be defrayed by the United States.

ARTICLE 6. In consideration of the past services and faithfulness of the Indian chief, Timothy, it is agreed that the United States shall appropriate the sum of six hundred dollars, to aid him in the erection of a house upon the lot of land which may be assigned to him, in accordance with the provisions of the third article of this treaty.

ARTICLE 7. The United States further agree, that the claims of certain members of the Nez Perce tribe against the government for services rendered and for horses furnished by them to the Oregon mounted volunteers, as appears by certificates issued by W. H. Fauntleroy, A. R. Qr. M. and Com. Oregon volunteers, on the 6th of March, 1856, at Camp Cornelius, and amounting to the sum of four thousand six hundred and sixty-five dollars, shall be paid to them in full, in gold coin.

ARTICLE 8. It is also understood that the aforesaid tribe do hereby renew their acknowledgments of dependence upon the government of the United States, their promises of friendship, and other pledges, as set forth in the eighth article of the treaty of June 11th, 1855; and further, that all the provisions of said treaty which are not abrogated or specifically changed by any article herein contained, shall remain the same to all intents and purposes as formerly, in the same obligations resting upon the United States, the same privileges continued to the Indians outside of the reservation, and the same rights secured to citizens of the U.S. as to right of way upon the streams and over the roads which may run through said reservation, as are therein set forth.

But it is further provided, that the United States is the only competent authority to declare and establish such necessary roads and highways, and that no other right is intended to be hereby granted to citizens of the United States than the right of way upon or over such roads as may thus be legally established: *Provided, however,* That the roads now usually traveled shall, in the mean time, be taken and deemed as within the meaning of this article, until otherwise enacted by act of Congress, or by the authority of the Indian department.

And the said tribe hereby consent, that upon the public roads which may run across the reservation there may be established, at such points as shall be necessary for public convenience, hotels or stage stands, of the number and necessity of which the agent or superintendent shall be the sole judge, who the same, with the privilege of using such amount of land for pasturage and other purposes connected with such establishment as the agent or superintendent shall deem necessary, it being understood that such lands for pasturage are to be enclosed, and the boundaries thereof described in the license.

And it is further understood and agreed that all ferries and bridges within the reservation shall be held and managed for the benefit of said tribe.

Such rules and regulations shall be made by the Commissioner of Indian Affairs, with the approval of the Secretary of the Interior, as shall regulate the travel on the highways, the management of the ferries and employed in any of the above relations, shall be subject to the control of the Indian department, and to the provisions of the act of Congress *"to regulate trade and intercourse with the Indian tribes, and to preserve peace on the frontiers."*

All timber within the bounds of the reservation is exclusively the property of the tribe, excepting that the U. S. government shall be permitted to use thereof for any purpose connected with its affairs, either in carrying out any of the provisions of this treaty, or in the maintaining of its necessary forts or garrisons.

The United States also agree to reserve all springs or fountains not adjacent to, or directly connected with, the streams or rivers within the lands hereby relinquished, and to keep back from settlement or entry so much of the surrounding land as may be necessary to prevent the said springs or fountains being enclosed; and, further, to preserve a perpetual right of way to and from the same, as watering places, for the use in common of both whites and Indians.

ARTICLE 9. Inasmuch as the Indians in council have expressed their desire that Robert Newell should have confirmed to him a piece of land lying between Snake and Clearwater rivers, the same having been given to him on the 9th day of June, 1861, and described in an instrument of writing bearing that date, and signed by several chiefs of the tribe, it is hereby agreed that the said Robert Newell shall receive from the United States a patent for the said tract of land.

ARTICLE 10. This treaty shall be obligatory upon the contracting parties as soon as the same shall be ratified by the President and Senate of the United States.

In testimony whereof the said C. H. Hale, superintendent of Indian affairs, and Charles Hutchins and S. D. Howe, United States Indian agents in the Territory of Washington, and the chiefs, headmen, and delegates of the aforesaid Nez Perce* tribe of Indians, have hereunto set their hands and seals at the place and on the day and year hereinbefore written.

Calvin H. Hale,
  Superintendent Indian Affairs, Wash. T.   [SEAL.]
Chas. Hutchins,
  United States Indian Agent, Wash. T.   [SEAL.]
S.D. Howe,
  United States Indian Agent, Wash. T.   [SEAL.]

Fa-Ind-7-1803 Lawyer,		We-as-cus, x	[SEAL.]
Head Chief Nez Perces Nation	[SEAL.]	Pep-hoom-kan, (Noah,) x	[SEAL.]
U-ute-sin-male-cun, x	[SEAL.]	Shin-ma-sha-ho-soot, x	[SEAL.]
Ha-harch-tuesta, x	[SEAL.]	Nie-ki-lil-meh-hoom, (Jacob,) x	[SEAL.]
Tip-ulania-timecca, x	[SEAL.]	Stoop-toop-nin, x	[SEAL.]

Es-coatum, x	[SEAL.]	Su-we-cus, x	[SEAL.]
Timothy, x	[SEAL.]	Wal-la-ta-mana, x	[SEAL.]
Levi, x	[SEAL.]	He-kaikt-il-pilp, x	[SEAL.]
Jason, x	[SEAL.]	Whis-tas-ket, x	[SEAL.]
Ip-she-ne-wish-kin, (Capt. John,) x	[SEAL.]	Neus-ne-keun, x	[SEAL.]
Weptas-jump-ki, x	[SEAL.]	Kul-lou-o-haikt, x	[SEAL.]
Kan-pow-e-een, x	[SEAL.]	Wow-en-am-ash-il-pilp, x	[SEAL.]
Watai-watai-wa-haikt, x	[SEAL.]	Tuck-e-tu-et-as, x	[SEAL.]
Kup-kup-pellia, x	[SEAL.]	Nic-a-las-in, x	[SEAL.]
Wap-tas-ta-mana, x	[SEAL.]	Was-atis-il-pilp, x	[SEAL.]
Peo-peo-ip-se-wat, x	[SEAL.]	Wow-es-en-at-im, x	[SEAL.]
Louis-in-ha-cush-nim, x	[SEAL.]	Hiram, x	[SEAL.]
Lam-lim-si-lilp-nim, x	[SEAL.]	Howlish-wampum, x	[SEAL.]
Tu-ki-lai-kish, x	[SEAL.]	Wat-ska-leeks, x	[SEAL.]
Sah-kan-tai, (Eagle,) x	[SEAL.]	Wa-lai-tus, x	[SEAL.]
We-ah-se-nat, x	[SEAL.]	Ky-e-wee-pus, x	[SEAL.]
Hin-mia-tun-pin, x	[SEAL.]	Ko-ko-il-pilp, x	[SEAL.]
Ma-hi-a-kim, x	[SEAL.]	Reuben, Tip-ia-la-na-uy-kala-tsekin, x	[SEAL.]
Shock-lo-turn-wa-haikt, (Jonah,) x	[SEAL.]	Wish-la-na-ka-nin, x	[SEAL.]
Kunness-tak-mal, x	[SEAL.]	Me-tat-ueptas, (Three Feathers,) x	[SEAL.]
Tu-lat-sy-wat-kin, x	[SEAL.]	Ray-kay-mass, x	[SEAL.]

APPENDIX 4

TREATY WITH THE NEZ PERCES, 1868

Whereas, certain amendments are desired by the Nez Perce tribe of Indians to their treaty concluded at the council-ground in the valley of Lapwai, in the Territory of Washington, on the 9th day of June, in the year of our Lord one thousand, eight hundred and sixty-three; and whereas the United States are willing to assent to said amendments, it is, therefore agreed by and between Nathaniel G. Taylor, commissioner on the part of the United States thereunto duly authorized, and Lawyer, Timothy and Jason, chiefs of said tribe, also being thereunto duly authorized, in manner and form following, that is to say:

ARTICLE 1. That all lands embraced within the limits of the tract set apart for the exclusive use and benefit of said Indians by the second article of said treaty of June 9, 1863, which are susceptible of cultivation and suitable for Indian farms, which are not now occupied by the United States for military purposes, or which are not required for agency or other buildings and purposes provided for by existing treaty stipulations, shall be surveyed as provided in the third article of said treaty of June 9, 1863, and as soon as the allotments shall be ploughed and fenced, and as soon as schools shall be established as provided by existing treaty stipulations, such Indians now residing outside the reservation as may be decided upon by the agent of the tribe and the Indians themselves, shall be removed to and located upon allotments within the reservation. Provided, however, that in case there should not be a sufficient quantity of suitable land within the boundaries of the reservation to provide allotments for those now there and those residing outside the boundaries of the same, then those residing outside, or as many thereof as allotments cannot be provided for, may remain upon the lands now occupied and improved by them. Provided that the land so occupied does not exceed

20 acres for each and every male person who shall have attained the age of 21 years, or is the head of a family, and the tenure of those remaining upon lands outside the reservation shall be the same as is provided in said third article of said treaty of June 9, 1863, for those receiving allotments within the reservation; and it is further agreed that those now residing outside of the boundaries of the reservation, and who may continue to so reside, shall be protected by the military authorities in their rights upon the allotments occupied by them, and also in the privilege of grazing their animals upon surrounding unoccupied lands.

ARTICLE 2. It is further agreed between the parties hereto that the stipulations contained in the eighth article of the treaty of June 9, 1863, relative to timber, are hereby annulled as far as the same provides that the United States shall be permitted no use thereof in the maintaining of forts or garrisons, and that the said Indians shall have the aid of the military authorities to protect the timber upon their reservation, and that none of the same shall be cut or removed without the consent of the head chief of the tribe, together with the consent of the agent and superintendent of Indian affairs first being given in writing, which written consent shall state the part of the reservation upon which the timber is to be cut, and also the quantity and the price to be paid therefore.

ARTICLE 3. It is further hereby stipulated and agreed that the amount due said tribe for school purposes, and for the support of teachers, that has not been expended for that purpose since the year 1864, but has been used for other purposes, shall be ascertained and the same shall be reimbursed to said tribe by appropriation by Congress, and shall be set apart and invested in United States bonds, and shall be held in trust by the United States, the interest on the same, to be paid to said tribe annually for the support of teachers.

In testimony whereof the said Commissioner on the part of the United States, and the said chiefs representing said Nez Perce tribe of Indians, have hereunto set their hands and seals this 13th day of August, in the year of our Lord one thousand eight hundred and sixty-eight, at the city of Washington, D.C.

N.G. Taylor,	[L.S.]
Commissioner Indian Affairs.	
Lawyer, Head Chief Nez Perces.	[L.S.]
Timothy, his x mark, Chief.	[L.S.]
Jason, his x mark, Chief.	[L.S.]

Appendix 5

The Dawes Act

An act to provide for the allotment of lands in severalty to Indians on the various reservations, and to extend the protection of the laws of the United States and the Territories over the Indians, and for other purposes.

Be it enacted by the Senate and House of Representatives of the United States of America in, Congress assembled, That in all cases where any tribe or band of Indians has been, or shall hereafter be, located upon any reservation created for their use, either by treaty stipulation or by virtue of an act of Congress or executive order setting apart the same for their use, the President of the United States be, and he hereby is, authorized, whenever in his opinion any reservation or any part thereof of such Indians is advantageous for agricultural and grazing purposes, to cause said reservation, or any part thereof, to be surveyed, or resurveyed if necessary, and to allot the lands in said reservation in severalty to any Indian located thereon in quantities as follows:

To each head of a family, one-quarter of a section;

To each single person over eighteen years of age, one-eighth of a section;

To each orphan child under eighteen years of age, one-eighth of a section, and

To each other single person under eighteen years now living, or who may be born prior to the date of the order of the President directing an allotment of the lands embraced in any reservation, one-sixteenth of a section: Provided, That in case there is not sufficient land in any of said reservations to allot lands to each individual of the classes above named in quantities as above provided, the lands embraced in such reservation or reservations shall be allotted to each individual of each of said classes pro rata in accordance with the provisions of this act: And provided further, That where the treaty or act of Congress setting apart such reservation provides the allotment of lands in severalty in quantities in excess of those herein provided, the President, in making allotments upon such reservation, shall allot the lands to each individual Indian belonging thereon in quantity as specified in such treaty or act: And provided further, That when the lands allotted are only valuable for grazing purposes, an additional allotment of such grazing lands, in quantities as above provided, shall be made to each individual.

SEC. 2. That all allotments set apart under the provisions of this act shall be selected by the Indians, heads of families selecting for their minor children, and the agents shall select for each orphan child, and in such manner as to embrace the improvements of the Indians making the selection where the improvements of two or more Indians have been made on the same legal subdivision of lands unless they shall otherwise agree, a provisional line may be run dividing said lands between them, and the amount to which each is entitled shall be equalized in the assignment of the remainder of the land to which they are entitled under this act: Provided, That if any one entitled to an allotment shall fail to make a selection within four years after the President shall direct that allotments may be made on a particular reservation, the Secretary of the Interior may direct the agent of such tribe or band, if such there be, and if there be no agent, then a special agent appointed for that purpose, to make a selection for such Indian, which selection shall be allotted as in cases where selections are made by the Indians, and patents shall issue in like manner.

SEC. 3. That the allotments provided for in this act shall be made by special agents appointed by the President for such purpose, and the agents in charge of the respective reservations on which the allotments are directed to be made, under such rules and regulations as the Secretary of the Interior may from time to time prescribe, and shall be certified by such agents to the Commissioner of Indian Affairs, in duplicate, one copy to be retained in the Indian Office and the other to be transmitted to the Secretary of the Interior for his action, and to be deposited in the General Land Office.

SEC. 4. That where any Indian not residing upon a reservation, or for whose tribe no reservation has been provided by treaty, act of Congress, or executive order, shall make settlement upon any surveyed or unsurveyed lands of the United States not otherwise appropriated, he or she shall be entitled, upon application to the local land-office for the district in which the lands are located, to have the same allotted to him or her, and to his or her children, in quantities and manner as provided in this act for Indians residing upon reservations; and when such settlement is made upon unsurveyed lands, the grant to such Indians shall be adjusted upon the survey of the lands so as to conform thereto; and patents shall be issued to them for such lands in the manner and with the restrictions as herein provided. And the fees to which the officers of such local land-office would have been entitled had such lands been entered under the general laws for the disposition of the public lands shall be paid to them, from any moneys in the Treasury of the United States not otherwise appropriated, upon a statement of an account in their behalf for such fees by the Commissioner of the General Land Office, and a certification of such account to the Secretary of the Treasury by the Secretary of the Interior.

SEC. 5. That upon the approval of the allotments provided for in this act by the Secretary of the Interior, he shall cause patents to issue therefore in the name of the allottees, which patents shall be of the legal effect, and declare that the United States does and will hold the land thus allotted, for the period of twenty-five years, in trust for the sole use and benefit of the Indian to whom such allotment shall have been made, or, in case of his decease, of his heirs according to the laws of the State or Territory where such land is located, and that at the expiration of said period the United States will convey the same by patent to said Indian, or his heirs as aforesaid, in fee, discharged of said trust and free of all charge or encumbrance whatsoever: Provided, That the President of the United States may in any case in his discretion extend the period. And if any conveyance shall be made of the lands set apart and allotted as herein provided, or any contract made touching the same, before the expiration of the time above mentioned, such conveyance or contract shall be absolutely null and void: Provided, That the law of descent and partition in force in the State or Territory where such lands are situate shall apply thereto after patents therefore have been executed and delivered, except as herein otherwise provided; and the laws of the State of Kansas regulating the descent and partition of real estate shall, so far as practicable, apply to all lands in the Indian Territory which may be allotted in severalty under the provisions of this act: And provided further, That at any time after lands have been allotted to all the Indians of any tribe as herein provided, or sooner if in the opinion of the President it shall be for the best interests of said tribe, it shall be lawful for the Secretary of the Interior to negotiate with such Indian tribe for the purchase and release by said tribe, in conformity with the treaty or statute under which such reservation is held, of such portions of its reservation not allotted as such tribe shall, from time to time, consent to sell, on such terms and conditions as shall be considered just and equitable between the United States and said tribe of Indians, which purchase shall not be complete until ratified by Congress, and the form and manner of executing such release prescribed by Congress: Provided however, That all lands adapted to agriculture, with or without irrigation so sold or released to the United States by any Indian tribe shall be held by the United States for the sole purpose of securing homes to actual settlers and shall be disposed of by the United States to actual and bona fide settlers only tracts not exceeding one hundred and sixty acres to any one person, on such terms as Congress shall prescribe, subject to grants which Congress may make in aid of education: And provided further, That no patents shall issue therefore except to the person so taking the same as and homestead, or his heirs, and after the expiration of five years occupancy thereof as such homestead, and any conveyance of said lands taken as a homestead, or any contract touching the same, or lieu thereon, created prior to the date of such patent, shall be null and void. And the sums agreed to be paid by the United States as purchase money for any portion of any such reservation shall be held in the Treasury of the United States for the sole use of the tribe or tribes Indians; to whom such reservations belonged; and the same, with interest thereon at three per cent per annum, shall be at all times subject to appropriation by Congress for the education and civilization of such tribe or tribes of Indians or the members thereof. The patents aforesaid shall be recorded in the General Land Office, and afterward delivered, free of charge, to the allottee entitled thereto. And if any religious society or other organization is now occupying any of the public lands to which this act is applicable, for religious or educational work among the Indians, the Secretary of the Interior is hereby authorized to confirm such occupation to such society or organization, in quantity not exceeding one hundred and sixty acres in any one tract, so long as the same shall be so occupied, on such terms as he shall deem just; but nothing herein contained shall change or alter any claim of such society for religious or educational purposes heretofore granted by law. And hereafter in the employment of Indian police, or any other employees in the public service among any of the Indian tribes or bands affected by this act, and where Indians can perform the duties required, those Indians who have availed themselves of the provisions of this act and become citizens of the United States shall be preferred.

SEC. 6. That upon the completion of said allotments and the patenting of the lands to said allottees, each and every member of the respective bands or tribes of Indians to whom allotments have been made shall have the benefit of and be subject to the laws, both civil and criminal, of the State or Territory in which they may reside; and no Territory shall pass or enforce any law denying any such Indian within its jurisdiction the equal protection of the law. And every Indian born within the territorial limits of the United States to whom allotments shall have been made under the provisions of this act, or under any law or treaty, and every Indian born within the territorial limits of the United States who has voluntarily taken up, within said limits, his residence separate and apart from any tribe of Indians therein, and has adopted the habits of civilized life, is hereby declared to be a citizen of the United States, and is entitled to all the rights, privileges, and immunities of such citizens, whether said Indian has been or not, by birth or otherwise, a member of any tribe of Indians within the territorial limits of the United States without in any manner affecting the right of any such Indian to tribal or other property.

SEC. 7. That in cases where the use of water for irrigation is necessary to render the lands within any Indian reservation available for agricultural purposes, the Secretary of the Interior be, and he is hereby, authorized to prescribe such rules and regulations as he may deem necessary to secure a just and equal distribution thereof among the Indians residing upon any such reservation; and no other appropriation or grant of water by any riparian proprietor shall be authorized or permitted to the damage of any other riparian proprietor.

SEC. 8. That the provisions of this act shall not extend to the territory occupied by the Cherokees, Creeks, Choctaws, Chickasaws, Seminoles, and Osage, Miamies and Peorias, and Sacs and Foxes, in the Indian Territory, nor to any of the reservations of the Seneca Nation of New York Indians in the State of New York, nor to that strip of territory in the State of Nebraska adjoining the Sioux Nation on the south added by executive order.

SEC. 9. That for the purpose of making the surveys and resurveys mentioned in section two of this act, there be, and hereby is, appropriated, out of any moneys in the Treasury not otherwise appropriated, the sum of one hundred thousand dollars, to be repaid proportionately out of the proceeds of the sales of such land as may be acquired from the Indians under the provisions of this act.

SEC. 10. That nothing in this act contained shall be so construed to affect the right and power of Congress to grant the right of way through any lands granted to an Indian, or a tribe of Indians, for railroads or other highways, or telegraph lines, for the public use, or condemn such lands to public uses, upon making just compensation.

SEC. 11. That nothing in this act shall be so construed as to prevent the removal of the Southern Ute Indians from their present reservation in Southwestern Colorado to a new reservation by and with consent of a majority of the adult male members of said tribe.

Approved, February, 8, 1887.

Appendix 6

1893 Allotment

AGREEMENT WITH THE NEZ PERCE INDIANS IN IDAHO.

SEC. 16. Whereas Robert Schleieher, James F. Allen, and Cyrus Beede, duly appointed commissioners on the part of the United States, did on the first day of May, eighteen hundred and ninety-three, conclude an agreement with the principal men and other male adults of the Nez Perce tribe of Indians upon the Lapwai Reservation, in the State of Idaho, which said agreement is as follows:

Whereas the President, under date of October thirty-first, eighteen hundred and ninety-two, and under the provisions of the Act of Congress entitled "An Act to provide for the allotment of lands in severalty to Indians on the various reservations, and to extend the protection of the laws of the United States and the Territories over the Indians, and for other purposes, approved February eighth, eighteen hundred and eighty-seven, authorized negotiations with the Nez Perce Indians in Idaho for the cession of their surplus lands; and

Whereas the said Nez Perce Indians are willing to dispose of a portion of the tract of land in the State of Idaho reserved as a home for their use and occupation by the second article of the treaty between said Indians and the United States, concluded June ninth, eighteen hundred and sixty-three:

Now, therefore, this agreement made and entered into in pursuance of the provisions of said Act of Congress approved February eighth, eighteen hundred and eighty-seven, at the Nez Perce Agency, by Robert Schleicher, James F. Allen, and Cyrus Beede, on the part of the United States, and the principal men and male adults of the Nez Perce tribe of Indians located on said Nez Perce Reservation, witnesseth:

ARTICLE I.

The said Nez Perce Indians hereby cede, sell, relinquish, and convey to the United States all their claim, right, title, and interest in and to all the unallotted lands within the limits of said reservation, saving, and excepting the following described tracts of lands, which are hereby retained by the said Indians, viz:

In township thirty-four, range four west: Northeast quarter, north half and southeast of northwest quarter, northeast quarter of southwest quarter, north half and east half of southwest quarter, and the southeast quarter of southeast quarter, section thirteen, four hundred and forty acres.

In township thirty-four, range three west: Sections ten; fifteen, thirty-six, one thousand nine hundred and twenty acres.

In township thirty-three, range three west: Section one; northwest quarter of northeast quarter, north half of northwest quarter section twelve, seven hundred and sixty acres.

In township thirty-five, range two west: South half of northeast quarter, northwest quarter, north half and southeast quarter of southwest quarter, southeast quarter section three; east half, east half of northwest quarter, southwest quarter section ten, section eleven; north half, north half of south half, section twenty-one; east half of northeast quarter, section twenty; sections twenty-two, twenty-seven, thirty-five, four thousand two hundred acres.

In township thirty-four, range two west: North half, southwest quarter, north half and southwest quarter and west half of southeast quarter of southeast quarter, section thirteen; section fourteen; north half section twenty-three, west half of east half and west half of northeast quarter, northwest quarter, north half of southwest quarter, west half of east half and northwest quarter and east half of southwest quarter of southeast quarter, section twenty-four; section twenty-nine, two thousand seven hundred acres.

In township thirty-three, range two west: West half and southeast quarter section six; sections sixteen, twenty-two, twenty-seven; north half and north half of south half section thirty-four, two thousand eight hundred and eighty acres.

In township thirty-four, range one west: West half section two; sections three, four: north half and southwest quarter section eight; north half section nine; north half and north half of southwest quarter section eighteen; northwest quarter section seventeen, two thousand nine hundred and sixty acres.

In township thirty-seven, range one east: Section twenty; section twenty-one, less south half of south half of southwest quarter of southeast quarter; (ten acre), one thousand two hundred and seventy acres.

In township thirty, six, range one east: South half of sections three, four; sections eleven, twelve, one thousand nine hundred and twenty acres.

In township thirty-six, range two east: Sections sixteen, seventeen, eighteen, twenty; all of section twenty-five west of boundary line of reservation; sections twenty-six, twenty-seven, four thousand two hundred and forty acres.

In township thirty-five, range two east: North half of sections sixteen, seventeen, section twenty-seven; north half of section thirty-four, one thousand six hundred acres.

In township thirty-four, range two east: East half and east half of west half of southeast quarter section twenty-four, one hundred acres.

In township thirty-four, range three east: South half of sections nineteen, twenty; north half; north half of south half; southwest quarter and north half of southeast quarter of southwest quarter; north half of south half or southeast quarter section twenty-three; north half; north half and north half of southwest quarter and southeast quarter of southwest quarter; southeast quarter section twenty-four; north half and southeast quarter of northeast quarter; north half of northwest quarter section twenty-five; south half of northeast quarter of northeast quarter section twenty-six; section twenty-nine; northeast quarter of northeast quarter and south half section thirty; northwest quarter and north half of southwest quarter section thirty-one; northeast quarter; north half and southeast quarter of northwest quarter section thirty-two; northwest quarter; north half of southwest quarter, section thirty-three, three thousand seven hundred acres.

In township thirty-three, range four east: South half of southeast quarter section eighteen; northeast quarter and fraction northeast of river in east half of northwest quarter section nineteen; fraction west of boundary line of reservation in section twenty-two; west half and southeast quarter of section thirty-five, one thousand four hundred and forty acres.

In township thirty-two, range four west: Fraction in west half of northeast quarter of southwest quarter; fraction in northwest quarter of southeast quarter section one; section two: south half of section six; west half and southeast quarter of northeast quarter of section nine, one thousand four hundred and ten acres.

In township thirty-one, range four west: South half of northeast quarter; southeast quarter of northwest quarter; northeast quarter of southwest quarter; southeast quarter section seventeen; northwest quarter section twenty-one, four hundred and eighty acres. Total, thirty-two thousand and twenty acres.

ARTICLE II.

It is also stipulated and agreed that the place known as ``the boom'' on the Clearwater River, near the mouth of Lapwai Creek, shall be excepted from this cession and reserved for the common use of the tribe, with full right of access thereto, and that the tract of land adjoining said boom, now occupied by James Moses, shall be allotted to him in such manner as not to interfere with such right. Also that there shall be reserved from said cession the land described as follows: "Commencing at a point at the margin of Clearwater River, on the south side thereof, which is three hundred yards below where the middle thread of Lapwai Creek empties into said river; run thence up the margin of said Clearwater River at low-water mark, nine hundred yards to a point; run thence south two hundred and fifty yards to a point; thence southwesterly, in a line to the southeast corner of a stone building, partly finished as a church; thence west three hundred yards to a point; thence from said point northerly in a straight line to the point of beginning; and also the adjoining tract of land lying southerly of said tract, on the south end thereof; commencing at the said corner of said church, and at the point three hundred yards west thereof, and run a line from each of said points. One of said lines running on the east side and the other on the west of said Lapwai Creek; along the foothills of each side of said creek; up the same sufficiently far so that a line being drawn east and west to intersect the aforesaid lines shall embrace within its boundaries, together with the first above described tract of land, a sufficient quantity of land as to include and comprise six hundred and forty acres;" for which described tracts of land the United States stipulates and agrees to pay to William G. Langford, his heirs or assigns, the sum of twenty thousand dollars, upon the execution by said Langford, his heirs or assigns, of a release and relinquishment to the United States of all right, title, interest, or claim, either legal or equitable, in and to said tracts of land, derived by virtue of a quit-claim deed of February fourteenth, eighteen hundred and sixty-eight, to the said William G. Langford, from Langdon S. Ward, treasurer of the American Board of Commissioners for Foreign Missions, which release and relinquishment shall be satisfactory to the Secretary of the Interior, and it is stipulated and agreed by said Nez Perce Indians that upon the execution and approval of such release and relinquishment the right of occupancy of said Indians in said described tracts shall terminate and cease and the complete title thereto immediately vest in the United States: Provided, That any member of the said Nez Perce tribe of Indians entitled to an allotment now occupying and having valuable improvements upon any of said lands not already occupied or improved by the United States may have the same allotted to him in such subdivisions as shall be prescribed and approved by the Secretary of the Interior, in lieu of an equal quantity of agricultural land allotted to him elsewhere; and for this purpose shall relinquish any patent that may have been issued to him before the title to said "Langford" tracts of land shall vest in the United States, and shall have a new patent issued to him of the form and legal effect prescribed by the fifth section of the act of February eighth, eighteen hundred and eighty-seven (twenty-fourth Statutes, three hundred and eighty-eight), covering the new allotment and that portion of the former allotment not surrendered. It is further agreed that five acres of said tract, upon which the Indian Presbyterian Church is located, as long as same shall remain a church, shall be patented to the trustees of said church; that the said five acres shall not include improvements made by the United States; the said five acres to be selected under the direction of the Commissioner of Indian Affairs.

ARTICLE III.

In consideration for the lands ceded, sold, relinquished, and conveyed as aforesaid the United States stipulates and agrees to pay to the said Nez Perce Indians the sum of one million six hundred and twenty-six thousand two hundred and twenty-two dollars, of which amount the sum of six hundred and twenty-six thousand two hundred and twenty-two dollars shall be paid to said Indians per capita as soon as practicable after the ratification of this agreement. The remainder of said sum of one million six hundred and twenty-six thousand two hundred and twenty-two dollars shall be deposited in the Treasury of the United States to the credit of the "Nez Perces Indians, of Idaho," and shall bear interest at the rate of five per centum per annum, which principal and interest shall be paid to said Indians per capita an follows, to wit: At the expiration of one year from the date of the ratification of this agreement the sum of fifty thousand dollars, and semiannually thereafter the sum of one hundred and fifty thousand dollars with the interest on the unexpended portion of the fund of one million dollars until the entire amount shall have been paid, and no part of the funds to be derived from the cession of lands by this agreement made shall be diverted or withheld from the disposition made by this article on account of any depredation or other act committed by any Nez Perce Indian, prior to the execution of this agreement, but the same shall be actually paid to the Indians in cash, in the manner and at the times as herein stipulated

ARTICLE IV.

It is further stipulated and agreed that the United States will purchase for the use of said Nez Perce Indians two portable steam saw mills, at a cost not exceeding ten thousand dollars, and will provide for said Indians, for a period not exceeding two years, and at a cost not exceeding twenty-four hundred dollars, a competent surveyor, for the purpose of fully informing said Indians as to the correct locations of their allotments and the corners.

ARTICLE V.

It is further stipulated and agreed that the lands by this agreement ceded, shall not be opened for public settlement until trust patents for the allotted lands shall have been duly issued and recorded, and the first payment shall have been made to said Indians.

ARTICLE VI.

It is further stipulated and agreed that any religious society or other organization now occupying under proper authority, for religious or educational work among the Indians, any of the lands ceded, shall have the right for two years from the date of the ratification of this agreement, within which to purchase the land so occupied, at the rate of three dollars per acre, the same to be conveyed to such society or organization by patent, in the usual form.

ARTICLE VII.

It is further stipulated and agreed that all allotments made to members of the tribe who have died since the same were made, or may die before the ratification of this agreement, shall be confirmed, and trust patents issued in the names of such allottees, respectively.

ARTICLE VIII.

It is further stipulated and agreed that the first per capita payment, provided for in Article VIII of this agreement, shall be made to those members of the Nez Perce tribe whose names appear on the schedule of allotments made by Special Agent Fletcher, and to such as may be born to them before the ratification of this agreement: Provided, That should it be found that any member of the tribe has been omitted from said schedule, such member shall share in the said payment, and shall be given an allotment, and each subsequent payment shall be made to those who receive the preceding payment and those born thereafter: Provided, That not more than one payment shall be made on account of a deceased member.

ARTICLE IX.

It is further agreed that the lands by this agreement ceded, those retained, and those allotted to the said Nez Perce Indians shall be subject, for a period of twenty-five years, to all the laws of the United States prohibiting the introduction of intoxicants into the Indian country, and that the Nez Perce Indian allottees, whether under the care of an Indian agent or not, shall, for a like period, be subject to all the laws of the United States prohibiting the sale or other disposition of intoxicants to Indians.

ARTICLE X.

Representation having been made by the Indians in council that several members of the Nez Perce tribe, to the number of about fifty, as per list hereto attached, served the United States under General O. O. Howard, in the late war with Joseph's Band of said tribe, as scouts, couriers, and messengers, and that they have received no pay therefore; it is agreed that the United States, through its properly constituted authority, will carefully examine each of the cases herewith presented, and make such remuneration to each of said claimants as shall, upon such examination, be found to be due; not exceeding the sum of two dollars and fifty cents per day each, for the time actually engaged in such service; it being understood and agreed that the time of service of said claimants in no case exceeded sixty days. And it also having been made to appear that Abraham Brooks, a member of the Nez Perce tribe of Indians, was engaged in the service of the United States in the late war with Joseph's Band of Nez Perces, and it also appearing that the said Abraham Brooks was wounded in said service, and that by reason thereof, he is now in failing health, and has been for several years; that he is now nearly blind in consequence thereof; it is agreed that an investigation of all the facts in the case shall be made by the proper authorities of the United States, as early as practicable, and that if found substantially as herein represented, or if found worthy under the law in such cases provided, he shall be allowed and paid by the United States a pension adequate to the service and disability.

ARTICLE XI.

The existing provisions of all former treaties with said Nez Perce Indians not inconsistent with the provisions of this agreement are hereby continued in full force and effect.

ARTICLE XII.

This agreement shall not take effect and be in force until ratified by the Congress of the United States.

In witness whereof the said Robert Schleicher, James F. Allen, and Cyrus Beede, on the part of the United States, and the principal men and other male adults of the Nez Perce tribe of Indians, have hereunto set their hands.

Concluded at the Nez Perce Agency, this first day of May, anno domini eighteen hundred and ninety-three.

ROBERT SCHLEICHER,
JAMES F. ALLEN,
CYRUS BEEDE.
A. B. LAWYER; and others.

Nez Perce tribal member Horace Axtell. (Photo courtesy of Antonio Smith.)

Appendix 7

Nez Perce Organization Chart 2002

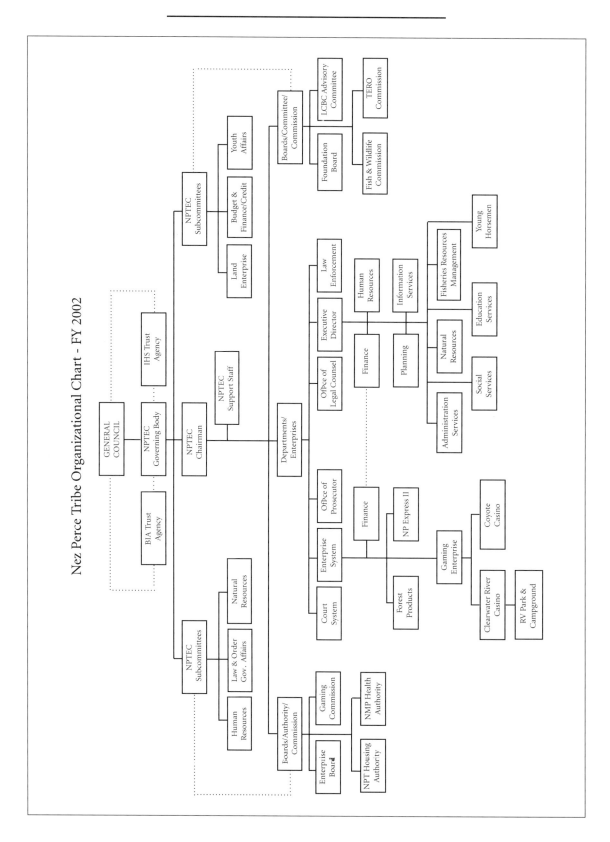

Nez Perce Tribe Organizational Chart - FY 2002

Glossary of Terms

Aboriginal Areas: This term is used today to describe the extensive historic and prehistoric lands occupied by a tribe and continuously used by the tribe to the exclusion of others.

Aboriginal Rights: Aboriginal rights are based on aboriginal title, original title, or Indian title. Title is the possessory right to occupy and to use an area of land that Indians have traditionally or historically used. Congress could extinguish such rights or title at will through a treaty or otherwise. Individual aboriginal rights were based on continuous actual possession by occupancy, enclosure, or other actions that established a right to the land to the exclusion of adverse claimants.

Abrogate: To abrogate means to cancel, repeal, or destroy. In *Lone Wolf v. Hitchcock*, 187 U.S. 553 (1903) the Supreme Court stated that Congress has the power to unilaterally abrogate tribal treaty rights.

Allotted Lands: The General Allotment Act of 1887 (Dawes Act, 24 Stat. 388) divided reservations into separate parcels to encourage individual Indians in agricultural pursuits and, ultimately, to open reservations to non-Indian settlement. Parcels allotted to tribal members were limited to 160 acres for each head of household (usually male) and to 80 acres for individual members. Any "remaining" acres were opened up to homesteaders. Under the Act, Indian-held lands declined from 138 million acres in 1887 to 48 million acres in 1934.

Bureau of Indian Affairs (BIA): The BIA is the principal federal agency responsible for carrying on the government-to-government relationship that exists between the United States and federally recognized tribes. The BIA also carries out the fiduciary responsibilities of the United States for tribes and their resources.

Ceded Lands: This term was first used in the Treaty with the Wyandot, Delaware, Ottawa, Chippewa, Pottawatamie, and Sac Nations of January 9, 1789 (7 Stat. 28). Since that time, many other treaties have referred to land cessions made by tribes to the United States. Most federal agencies and Indian tribes prefer to use the term "ceded lands" to describe areas ceded, sold, relinquished, or conveyed to the United States when the treaties were signed or when reservation lands were established. Ceded lands were defined in 1978 by the U.S. Court of Claims, which held that "only lands actually owned by a tribe can be ceded to the U.S."

Co-Management: This term refers to two or more entities, each having legally established management responsibility, working together to actively protect, conserve, enhance, or restore lands and natural resources.

Cultural Resources: This term refers to those things that the Nez Perce deem important for the perpetuation of their culture.

Indian: This term refers to an individual who is recognized by a tribe, band, or community as a member. Tribal membership requirements can be established by usage, written law, treaty, or intertribal agreement. Membership is typically defined by a tribal constitution, tribal law, or a tribal roll; membership requirements can vary from tribe to tribe. One tribe, for example may require higher or lower degrees of blood quantum, than another.

Indian Claims Commission: Congress established this special commission in 1946 to hear and resolve claims against the federal government under the Indian Claims Commission Act of 1946 (60 Stat. 1049). The statute of limitations, which would normally apply (and which would bar suits for old claims) was waived by the Commission, which was authorized to hear only those tribal claims filed before 13 August 1951, or those claims that had accrued prior to enactment of the Commission.

Indian Country: 18 U.S.C. § 1151 defines Indian Country as follows: Indian country includes all lands within boundaries of an Indian reservation, regardless of ownership. Therefore, land located within a reservation, but owned by a non-Indian, is Indian Country. Even rights-of-way through reservation lands, such as state or federal highways, remain a part of Indian Country. When the federal government sets aside land under federal supervision for Indians, the land becomes Indian Country.

Indian Country also includes "all dependent Indian communities" within the United States. A dependent Indian community is any area of land that has been set aside by the federal government for the use, occupancy, or benefit of Indians, even if the area of land is not a part of a reservation. The Pueblos of New Mexico, whose lands are owned by the tribes themselves but are under federal supervision, provide an example. Other examples include tribal housing projects located on federal lands or federally operated boarding schools.

Indian Title: The concept of Indian Title gave European nations title over tribal lands only as these European nations were opposed to one another, but use and occupancy of the lands were retained by the tribes. Tribes retain the sole right of use and of occupancy of lands until acquired by "purchase or by conquest." Once Indian title is extinguished, lands become reservations or ceded territory.

Manifest Destiny: This term refers to 19th century view that the United States was predestined to expand across the North American continent, regardless of the wishes of its original inhabitants. Manifest Destiny is said to have been satisfied when the United States was able to acquire enough land to span the geographical distance between the Atlantic and the Pacific coasts.

North Central Idaho Jurisdictional Alliance: This term refers to a coalition of non-tribal governmental entities within the reservation that wants to diminish tribal sovereignty and the existence of the Nez Perce Reservation.

Reserved Rights Doctrine: The doctrine describes the legal concept that tribes retain the rights associated with use and occupancy of their lands unless they are expressly given up. Many tribes, including the Nez Perce Tribe, have explicitly reserved both on and off reservation fishing, hunting, gathering, and grazing rights as well as implicit water rights.

Reservation: A reservation is an area over which a tribe exercises its sovereign authority. Typically, a reservation is reserved and described by a tribe in a treaty, executive order, or other agreement.

Sovereign: This term refers to a body of persons or a nation having independent and self-governing power, status, or authority. The Supreme Court has described tribes as distinct, self-governing political entities, but dependent upon the United States as their trustee. Tribes are described as "domestic dependent nations."

Sovereignty: This term refers to the inherent right of a tribe to govern all actions within its own jurisdiction based upon traditional systems and laws that arise from the people themselves. Sovereignty includes the right of tribes to live freely and to develop socially, economically, culturally, spiritually, and politically. Tribal sovereignty has two principal attributes: (1) Tribes possess inherent governmental power over all internal affairs and (2) States are precluded from interfering with the Tribes' self-government.

Steal Treaty: This term refers to the Treaty of 1863. After gold and other metals were discovered within the original 1855 Nez Perce Reservation, the United States negotiated a new treaty with the Tribe that stripped the Nez Perce of the Wallowa and Imnaha Valleys and the land at the confluence of the Snake and Clearwater Rivers (the sites of the present-day towns of Lewiston, Idaho, and Clarkston, Washington).

Treaty: A treaty is a binding, legal agreement between two or more sovereign nations. Treaties have been in existence as long as nations. Treaties have also been called "alliances," "compacts," "conventions," "acts," "contracts," and "agreements." Treaties are made between sovereigns to establish a mutual understanding and agreement. Usually, the subject matter of treaties relates to one or more of the following: (1) peace and friendship, (2) military alliances, (3) boundaries or real estate, and (4) trade.

Treaty Territory: This term is used to describe the geographic area over which a tribe exercises treaty-reserved rights. For the Nez Perce Tribe, this is the area where tribal members exercise treaty-reserved hunting, fishing, gathering, and grazing rights. Nez Perce Treaty Territory includes areas in Idaho, Oregon, Washington, and Montana.

Tribe: This legal term applies to a group or groups of indigenous people of North America. A tribe is usually composed of a racial, political, or social group comprising numerous families, villages, or the like and having a common language, culture, and, often, ancestry.

Trust Land: Trust Land refers to any land in collective tribal holding or individual tribal member ownership for which the Secretary of the Interior has a continuing trust responsibility to manage. The United States holds the land in trust for the benefit of the respective tribe or individual. Trust lands are subject to alienation (sale, transfer, or other loss) only with the approval of the United States and cannot be taxed by state or local governments.

Usual and Accustomed: This treaty term describes lands where a tribe usually traveled or was accustomed to travel for the purposes of fishing, hunting, gathering, or grazing. Usual and accustomed fishing places exist both on and off the reservation and are not limited to a tribe's ceded lands. For the Nez Perce Tribe, usual and accustomed fishing areas extend as far west as Portland and as far east as Montana.

SELECTED BIBLIOGRAPHY

SIGNIFICANT COURT DECISIONS

The following cases have shaped federal Indian law by establishing tribes as sovereign governments or limiting tribal powers as indicated.

JOHNSON V. MCINTOSH, 21 U.S. 543, 5 L.ED. 681 (1823)

In this first case in which the Supreme Court set forth its opinion on the issue of the relationship of Indian tribes and their legal and historical relation to the land, the court ruled that tribes had original Indian title or a "right of occupancy," but that original title was subject to the discovering nation. Therefore, the Court concluded a transfer of land from an Indian tribe to a private individual is invalid unless approved by the United States.

CHEROKEE NATION V GEORGIA, 30 U.S. (5 PET.) 1, 8 L.ED. 25 (1831)

The Supreme Court held that although the Cherokee Tribe succeeded in demonstrating that it was a "state" capable of managing its own affairs, the Tribe could not be considered a "foreign state" for the purposes of filing suit against Georgia. The Court instead characterized tribes as "domestic dependent nations."

WORCESTER V. GEORGIA, 31 U.S. (6 PET.) 515, 8 L.ED. 483 (1832)

A conviction by the State of Georgia against missionaries who were proselytizing on Cherokee lands was reversed by the U.S. Supreme Court on the basis that "the Cherokee nation. . .is a distinct community, occupying its own territory, with boundaries accurately described, in which the laws of Georgia can have no force."

UNITED STATES V. 43 GALLONS OF WHISKEY, 93 U.S. 188 (1876)

In this case, the sovereign status of Indian tribes was recognized by the United States as it had been even earlier by foreign governments that had entered into treaties with Tribes. Treaties, by definition, are agreements between sovereign governments. Indian treaties are accorded the same dignity as that given to treaties with foreign nations.

UNITED STATES V. TAYLOR, (1877)

The Supreme Court of the Washington Territory ordered Taylor to remove the obstruction that blocked the Yakama Indians from fishing one of their "usual and accustomed" places.

UNITED STATES V. KAGAMA, 118 U.S. 375, 6 S.CT. 1109 (1886)

The Supreme Court upheld federal jurisdiction in Indian Country through the Major Crimes Act, stating that "[Indian] communities are dependent on the United States. . . ."

Lone Wolf v. Hitchcock, 187 U.S. 553, 23 S.Ct. 216 (1903)

In this case (involving the sale of tribal lands) the court reiterated the plenary authority of Congress over the Tribes, and upheld a federal statutory process for such sale.

United States v. Winans, 198 U.S. 371, 25 S.Ct. 662, 49 L.Ed. 1089 (1905)

In this case, the Supreme Court upheld a Yakama tribal member's right to a treaty related easement over private lands to access traditional fishing places and exercise his right to fish. The Court held that the rights contained in the 1855 Treaty, another Stevens Treaty, were not a grant of rights to the Tribe, but rather was a reservation of rights already held by the Tribe. The Court stated, "(T)he treaty was not a grant of rights to the Indians, but a grant of rights from them – a reservation of those not granted." This is referred to as the "reserved rights doctrine."

Winters v. U.S., 207 U.S. 564, 28 S.Ct. 207, 52 L.Ed. 340 (1908)

Fort Belknap Reservation in Montana was created in 1888 by Executive Order. The 1888 Agreement described the northern boundary of the reservation as the middle of the Milk River. The Supreme Court found that the intent of the 1888 Agreement was to help the Tribes become "pastoral and civilized" and develop the lands agriculturally and therefore that the Tribe reserved sufficient water to meet the purposes of the Reservation. This case established the "reserved water rights doctrine."

United States v. Sandoval, 231 U.S. 28, 34 S.Ct. 1 (1913)

The Pueblos of New Mexico were deemed to be "Indian Country," although their lands were held in fee simple under Spanish grants and were not formally designated as reservations. Since the Pueblos were wards dependent upon the federal government's guardianship, the court considered Pueblo lands to be Indian lands.

Blackfeet, et al. Nations v. United States, 81 C.Cls. 101 (1935)

The treaty of 17 October 1855, creating rights of several tribes, including the Nez Perce, in the "common hunting ground" located on the Blackfeet Indian reservation, created "permissive" rights, which included no obligation on the part of the United States to maintain the game supply, but did obligate the United States to protect the hunting tribes from interference from other tribes.

Tulee v. Washington, 315 U.S. 681, 62 S.Ct. 862, 86 L.Ed. 1115 (1942)

Supreme Court held that tribal members exercising their treaty reserved right to fish at usual and accustomed fish areas were not required to buy state fishing license.

State v. McConville, 65 Idaho 46, 139 P.2d 485 (Idaho 1943)

John McConville, a Nez Perce Tribal member, was arrested for fishing without a state fishing license. The Idaho Supreme Court upheld a tribal member's right to fish on and off reservation without the requirement of a state license on the basis of the treaty rights reserved to him and that the right was never abrogated.

State v. Arthur, 74 Idaho 251, 261 P.2d 135 (Idaho 1953)

David Arthur, a Nez Perce tribal member, was charged by the State with killing a deer out of season when he shot a deer outside the reservation boundary on National Forest lands. The Idaho Supreme Court determined that a member of the Nez Perce Tribe has a right to hunt on open and unclaimed lands, such as National Forest lands, at any time free of state regulation.

Sohappy v. Smith, 302 F.Supp. 899 (1969)

The federal court limited the State of Oregon's power to regulate the exercise of the Indians' federal treaty right to fish in that regulation must be (1) necessary for conservation of the fish; (2) the state restrictions must not discriminate against the Indians; and (3) they must meet appropriate standards.

U.S. v. Washington, 384 F.Supp. 312 (W.D. 1974) (Boldt Decision)

Judge George Boldt held that the Stevens Treaty grants tribes the right to harvest up to 50% of the fish that would return to the Tribes' usual and accustomed fishing places.

Montana v. U.S. 450 U.S. 544, 101 S.Ct. 1245, 67 L.Ed.2d 493 (1981)

The Supreme Court held that the Crow Tribe's authority to regulate hunting and fishing extended only to lands where the Tribe exercises exclusive control. The Court stated that tribes have the authority to regulate the conduct of non-Indians when there is a consensual relationship with the tribe or such conduct threatens the economic, political, or general welfare of the tribe.

Sohappy v. Hodell, (1990)

The court recognized that a tribe's treaty-reserved rights include the ability to erect structures at "usual and accustomed" fishing sites.

Lower Brule Sioux Tribe v. Ada Deer, 911 F. Supp. 395 (1995)

In this case the court ordered that Reduction In Force (RIF) notices issued to Bureau of Indian Affairs (BIA) employees at Lower Brule Agency are invalid due to the BIA's failure to afford the Tribe meaningful, prior consultation pursuant to BIA policies and guidelines.

Klamath Tribes v. United States, 24 ILR 3017 (D.Or. 1996)

The Court in this case prohibited the federal defendants from proceeding with salvage logging without ensuring in consultation with the Klamath Tribe, on a government-to-government basis, that the resources on which the Tribe's treaty rights depend would be protected.

Strate v. A-1 Contractors, 520 U.S. 438, 117 S.Ct. 1404, 137 L.Ed.2d 661 (1997)

Supreme Court held that when an accident occurred on a portion of public highway maintained by the state under federally granted right-of-way over reservation land, tribal courts lacked civil jurisdiction against the allegedly negligent driver and the driver's employer, neither of whom was a member of tribe, absent a statute or treaty authorizing the tribe to govern conduct of nonmembers on the highway in question.

County of Lewis v. Allen, 163 F.3d 509 (9ᵀᴴ Cir. 1998)

Ninth Circuit Court of Appeals held that Nez Perce Tribal Court lacked jurisdiction over tort action of a tribal member against the county and its law enforcement officers, claiming false arrest, other torts, and a civil rights violation stemming from an allegedly invalid arrest. The court found that the tribal court lacked jurisdiction to adjudicate the claims because the Tribe divested itself of exclusive sovereignty over law enforcement activities as the result of a law enforcement agreement between the Tribe and the State of Idaho. This agreement has since been rescinded by the Nez Perce Tribal Executive Committee.

State of Washington v. Buchanan, (1999)

This case dealt with tribal hunting areas within ceded lands. The court recognized that hunting rights may extend outside a tribe's ceded territory where there is evidence that the tribe's aboriginal hunting grounds extended outside the ceded territory.

U.S. v. Webb, 219 F.3d 1127 (9ᵀᴴ Cir. 2000)

The Ninth Circuit Court of Appeals held that Congress, in ratifying the 1893 Agreement with the Nez Perce, did not intend to terminate or diminish the reservation and that the United States, as opposed to the State of Idaho, retained criminal jurisdiction over the criminal acts of a tribal member.

Atkinson Trading v. Shirley, 531 U.S. 1009, 121 S.Ct. 1825, 149 L.Ed.2d 889 (2001)

The Supreme Court held that the Navajo Tribe lacked authority to impose tax on non-member guests of a hotel owned by a non-member but located within boundaries of Navajo Reservation.

Nevada v. Hicks, 533 U.S. 353, 121 S.Ct. 2304, 150 L.Ed.2d 398 (2001)

The Supreme Court held that the Fallon Paiute-Shoshone Tribal Court did not have jurisdiction to adjudicate tribal member's civil rights claims and tort action filed against State officials arising from execution of a search warrant on tribal land within the reservation for evidence of an off-reservation poaching crime. The Court held that the test of jurisdiction established in *Montana v. U.S.* applies on tribal lands.

U.S. v. Oregon (District of Oregon) — Ongoing Litigation

U.S. v. Oregon, originally a combination of two cases, *Sohappy v. Smith* and *U.S. v. Oregon* (302 F. Supp. 899), legally upheld the Columbia River treaty tribes reserved fishing rights. Although the Sohappy case was closed in 1978, *U.S. v. Oregon* remains under the federal court's continuing jurisdiction serving to protect the tribe's treaty reserved fishing rights.

In his 1969 decision, Judge Robert C. Belloni ruled that state regulatory power over Indian fishing is limited because, in 1855 treaties between the United States and the

Nez Perce, Umatilla, Warm Springs, and Yakama tribes, these tribes had reserved rights to fish at "all usual and accustomed" places whether on or off reservation.

Snake River Basin Adjudication (Idaho State District Court) — Ongoing Litigation

The Snake River Basin Adjudication (SRBA) involves the Snake River and all of its tributaries encompassing most of the state. It is an Idaho state court proceeding to conclusively adjudicate all water rights in the Snake River Basin, amounting to over 170,000 claims. The Nez Perce Tribe has water claims on and off-reservation to protect fish habitat (instream flows), claims to use of springs and fountains within the former 1855 Reservation, as well as on-reservation claims for consumptive use (agriculture and municipal uses).

We list here only the writings that we have used in the making of this book. This list is by no means, however, a complete record of the works and sources we have consulted. It merely indicates the substance and range of reading upon which we have formed our ideas, and we intend it to serve only as a convenience for those who wish to pursue the subjects of Nez Perce treaties and Nez Perce history.

Baird, Dennis W., Diane Mallickan, W.R. Swagerty. eds. *The Nez Perce Nation Divided: Firsthand Accounts of Events Leading to the 1863 Treaty*. Moscow: University of Idaho Press., 2002.

Baird, Dennis W., ed. *Reports on the Aftermath of the 1863 Nez Perce Treaty by Chief Lawyer, Governor Caleb Lyon, General Benjamin Alvord and Indian Agent James O'Neill*. University of Idaho Library Northwest Historical Manuscript Series. Moscow: University of Idaho Library, 1999.

Baird, Dennis W., ed. *With Bird and Truax on the Lolo Trail: Building the Virginia City to Lewiston Wagon Road, 1865-1867*. University of Idaho Library Northwest Historical Manuscript Series. Moscow: University of Idaho Library, 1999.

Beal, Merril D. *I Will Fight No More Forever: Chief Joseph and the Nez Perce War*. Seattle: University of Washington Press, 1963.

Canby, William C. *American Indian Law*. St. Paul: West Publishing Company, 1998.

Cohen, Felix S. *Handbook of Federal Indian Law*. Charlottesville, Virgrinia: The Michie Company Law Publishers, 1982.

Gay, E. Jane. *With the Nez Perces: Alice Fletcher in the Field, 1889-92*. Lincoln: University of Nebraska Press, 1981.

Getches, D.H., C.F. Wilkinson, and R.A. Williams Jr. *Cases and Materials on Federal Indian Law*, 3rd Edition, St. Paul: West Publishing Company, 1993.

Grafe, L. Steven. "Still They Look Handsome: The Spalding-Allen Collection." *American Indian Art Magazine*, Summer 1997.

Johnson, Lyndon B. 4 Weekly Comp. Presidential Document. 10 (1968). President, Proclamation, "Proclamation 5242, Amending etc. 15.363 in Chicago

Josephy. Alvin M. Jr. *The Nez Perce Indians and the Opening of the Northwest.* Abridged Edition. Lincoln: University of Nebraska Press, 1965.

Kappler, Charles J. ed. *Indian Affairs, Laws and Treaties.* Washington: Government Printing Office, 1904

Landeen, Dan, A. Pinkham. *Salmon and His People: Fish and Fishing in Nez Perce Culture.* Lewiston, Idaho: Confluence Press, 1999.
Mallickan, Diane. Introduction to *Memorial of the Nez Perce Indians Residing in the State of Idaho to the Congress of the United States.* Presented by Mr. Borah. Compiled by Starr J. Maxwell. Moscow: University of Idaho Library Northwest Historical Manuscript Series. Moscow: University of Idaho Library, 2000.

Mazurek, Joseph P., ed. *American Indian Law Deskbook: Conference of Western Attorney's General.* Niwot: University Press of Colorado, 1998.

Memorial of the Nez Perce Indians Residing in the State of Idaho to the Congress of the United States. Presented by Mr. Borah. Compiled by Starr J. Maxwell. Moscow: University of Idaho Library Northwest Historical Manuscript Series. Moscow: University of Idaho Library, 2000.

McWhorter, Lucullus V. 1952. *Hear Me My Chiefs.* Caldwell, Idaho: Caxton Printers, Ltd.

McWhorter, Lucullus V. *Yellow Wolf: His Own Story.* Caldwell, Idaho: Caxton Printers, Ltd., 1940.

Pevar, Stephen L. *The Rights of Indians and Tribes: The Basic ACLU Guide to Indian and Tribal Rights.* Carbondale: Southern Illinois Press, 1992.

Seufert F.A. *Wheels of Fortune.* Portland: Oregon Historical Society, 1980.

Swagerty, W.R. "Nez Perce Voices." Manuscript.

United States Department of Agriculture. *Forest Service National Resource Book on American Indian and Alaska Native Relations*, 1997.

U.S. Department of the Interior. Bureau of Indian Affairs. Certified Copy of the Original Minutes of the Official Proceedings at the Council in Walla Walla Valley, Which Culminated in the Stevens Treaty of 1855. Portland, Oregon: Bureau of Indian Affairs, 1953. (Copy of original minutes on file in the National Archives).